★ THE AMERICAN ADVENTURE SERIES ★

FUR TRAPPERS OF THE OLD WEST

BY

A. M. ANDERSON

Illustrated by
JACK MERRYWEATHER

WHEELER PUBLISHING COMPANY

CHICAGO

THE AMERICAN ADVENTURE SERIES

△

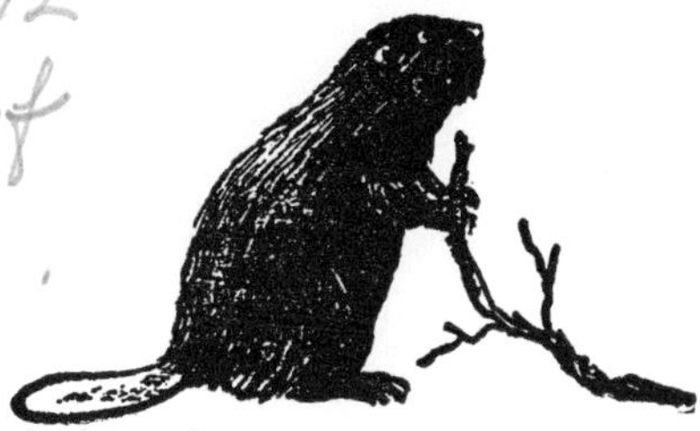

Table of Contents

THE FUR TRAPPERS *of the Old West were fearless, daring men. They knew the West when it was a wilderness — a land of Indians and sudden death. Following the countless beaver streams these bold, buckskin-clad men explored the wilderness until it held no secrets from them.*

This is more than a story of the fur trade and the adventures shared by the trappers. It is also a story of the trails they blazed for the settlers of a young, growing America.

A. M. ANDERSON

Headed for the Wilderness

YOUNG Jim Bridger shouldered his rifle and started down a street leading to the river. The long fringe on his buckskin clothes flapped softly as he strode along. His moccasins made no sound on the wooden sidewalk.

The sun was just rising over the little frontier town of St. Louis. Even at this early hour most of the stores and trading posts were already open.

As Jim passed a trading post a man called, "Hey, young fellow, are you heading west this morning with Ashley and Henry?"

"Yes, I am," replied Jim. "I've signed up to trap for the Rocky Mountain Fur Company."

"Good luck and look out for the Indians."

"The Indians won't get my hair," laughed Jim, waving his rifle. He strode on whistling.

Near the river Jim stopped in front of a gun shop. A weather-beaten sign over the open door swung back and forth in the April breeze.

Inside the shop an old man was seated at a workman's bench. He was mending a gun. Without looking up he said, "Come in, Jim."

"Good morning, Old John," greeted Jim as he entered the shop. "How did you know I was coming down the street?"

"Your whistling is always a little off key." Old John laughed, but his faded blue eyes had a merry twinkle. "Well, Jim, this is your big day," he added. "Turn around and let me see how the clothes we made fit you."

Jim laughed and tossed his head. His long, dark hair fell back over his shoulders. His buckskin clothes did not fit very well, but Jim's pride in his new outfit made Old John smile.

Old John studied Jim and admired the easy grace of his quick movements. Jim was only eighteen years old, but he was tall, well over six feet. He was slim, strong, and straight as an arrow. His clear gray eyes were keen and searching.

"What kind of knife is that you have in your belt?" Old John asked. "It doesn't look like a strong one to me. Where did you get it?"

"I bought it at a trading post," answered Jim. "It isn't a very good one, but it is the best I could afford to buy."

Old John rose from his bench and walked slowly across the shop to a chest of drawers. He unlocked a drawer and opened it. He held up a trapper's knife.

"An Indian or a grizzly bear isn't going to wait for you to afford a good knife," he said. "Here, take this one."

"I can't take it," protested Jim. "You have done too much for me already."

"Take it, Jim. I want you to have it."

Jim looked at the old man for a minute. Then he reached out and took the knife. "Thank you, Old John," he said simply.

Jim ran his fingers along the keen blade of steel and over the sturdy, wooden handle. "Why, it's a Green River knife!" he exclaimed. "That's the best knife money can buy."

"Yes, it is," agreed Old John. "It's named after a river somewhere in the West. Only a few white men have seen the river. They say it flows through a beautiful valley. Maybe some day you will see the Green River Valley and—"

"Maybe I'll see rivers and valleys no other white man has ever seen before," broke in Jim. "And maybe I'll explore lands that even the Indians have not explored. That's why I want to be a trapper, Old John. I don't want to spend my life working in a blacksmith shop. I don't want to listen to the adventures of other men. I want to see the West myself. I want to live my own adventures."

"Of course you do, Jim. I wish I were going with you." Old John sighed. "You have a whole life of adventure ahead of you. Here I am—old, feeble, tied to a workman's bench—and I used to be a fur trapper."

"Then you still think I was right in giving up my job?"

"I certainly do! This is your chance to become a fur trapper—a mountain man. There is nothing like it in all the world. You'll starve and freeze and fight Indians and you'll love it."

"I know I will," said Jim.

"Are you going up the river on the keelboats," asked Old John, "or are you riding with the men of the land party?"

"I'll be on one of the keelboats. So will Tom Fitzpatrick. He's waiting for me on the river front."

"I'm glad you will be with Tom. He's a fine young man. He's only a few years older than you, but he has had some experience as a trapper. I hear he's a good one. The men speak well of him."

As they were talking a rough-looking man entered the shop. In a loud voice he ordered, "Old John, mend my gun at once!"

Old John examined the gun and said, "I can mend it, but you will have to wait."

"I want it done now!"

"I'm working on a trapper's gun. I must have it ready for him in an hour. Why don't you take it to the shop across the street?"

"I told you to mend my gun. Do you understand?"

"Yes, I understand, but I can't do it now."

"Maybe this will get you started." The man

slapped Old John across the face. "Now get busy!"

Jim, standing a short distance away, stepped quickly to Old John and took the gun from him. Turning to the man he said, "Old John told you to take your gun to another shop. Now take it and get out!"

"Stay out of this, kid," sneered the man.

"I said, 'Get out!'"

"Jim!" warned Old John, "he's reaching for his knife."

Before the man could strike, Jim grabbed him by the arm and twisted it. The knife fell to the floor. With a swift kick Jim sent it across the floor and out through the open door.

"Now get out!" said Jim.

"I'll get you for this!" the man called back over his shoulder.

Jim made no reply.

"You shouldn't have done that, Jim," said Old John. "He will get even with you."

"I'm not afraid of him," laughed Jim, "and I'm leaving St. Louis anyway."

"Don't you know who he is?"

"No, Old John, and I don't care who he is."

"Jim, that was Wolf Andrews."

"Wolf Andrews, the Indian fighter?"

"Yes, and he is going with Ashley. General Ashley doesn't like Wolf Andrews. But Wolf is an expert trapper and Indian fighter. Such men are hard to find, so Ashley had to sign him up for this trip. Watch out for him!"

"Don't worry. I can take care of myself." Jim held out his hand. "Good-by, Old John. You have been like a father to me. I'll never forget you. Thanks for everything."

"I don't want any thanks. But there is one thing I do ask of you, Jim. Be a man—a real man. That's all. Good-by, son."

A few minutes later Jim was on the river front. The river landing was lined with boats of every kind used on the Mississippi and other western rivers and streams. Light Indian canoes tossed up and down in the water next to the clumsy, but strongly built, flatboats. Heavy barges lay beside dugouts hollowed out of big trees. Several steamboats were tied to the pier. They were the newest boats on the Mississippi and men always crowded around them.

Most of the boats, however, were the long, graceful keelboats. They were about eighty feet long and eighteen feet wide. They were popular because they were sturdy, but lightly built. Even when heavily loaded they floated high in the water. They could be poled up the rivers. But when the water was too deep, a land party had to pull the boats with a long cordelle, or towing rope. When the wind was favorable, sails could be used.

A group of men were gathered near the spot where Ashley's keelboats were tied to the landing. Jim looked about for Tom. He recognized his tall, black-haired friend and hurried forward.

"Hello, Tom!" he called.

Tom waved his big, black felt hat. "Hello, Jim!" he answered. There was a touch of Irish laughter in his strong voice.

"Are you ready to leave?" he asked as Jim joined him.

"I'm ready," Jim replied.

Shortly after sunrise the people of the little

frontier town began coming down to the river.
Young mothers, with babies in their arms, came
with their trapper husbands. Children ran about
playing and enjoying the excitement of the crowd.
The women were quiet, trying to hide their fears.
They knew the West was a wilderness, a land of
Indians and sudden death.

"Here they come!" a man shouted.

General William Ashley, a handsome, command-
ing man, and his able partner of the new fur
company, Major Andrew Henry, waved their hats
to the crowd. The two buckskin-clad men hurried
up the gangplank of the leading keelboat and
disappeared into the cabin.

Jim, Tom, and twenty-two other men were ordered to board the keelboat. Each man was given
an iron-tipped pole about twenty feet long. The
men were told to take their places, half on one
side and half on the opposite side of the boat. Jim
and Tom hurried down the narrow catwalk on
the boat to their places.

"Set poles!" the keelboat captain shouted.

Each man dipped his pole into the muddy water

and pushed the iron-tipped end firmly into the river bottom. Then holding the pole against one shoulder he braced himself by placing his feet against the cleats, or strips of wood, nailed to the catwalk.

"Down on your poles!"

Pushing on his pole each man slowly walked to the stern of the boat. Cleat by cleat he made his way along the catwalk straining his muscles with every step. Slowly—slowly the boat slipped from the landing.

When a man reached the stern of the boat, he pulled his pole from the water and ran forward to the head of the line. Then he reset his pole against the river bottom. Again he braced himself and again step by step he walked to the stern.

With twenty-four polers on a keelboat there were eighteen men pushing while six men were hurrying from the stern to the head of the line.

The land party of fifty men guided their horses along the river bank. They were ready to tow a boat if it ran onto a sand bar, a snag, or when the water was too deep.

Jim looked back at the second keelboat just heading upstream. "We're on our way," he said to himself. "At last I'm going to see the West."

Jim, Tom, and the other polers were all powerfully built men and they were used to hard work. But poling a keelboat was a back-breaking job.

"Ashley says that each day the men on the boats are to exchange places with the men of the land party," said Tom rubbing his big hands. "So tomorrow we'll be with the land party."

"Good," laughed Jim. "Riding a horse will suit me better than pushing on this pole. I know we're headed for Three Forks on the Missouri River, but how far is it from here?"

"About two thousand miles."

"How long will it take us to get there?"

"Well, it's April now." Tom hesitated. "We ought to get there sometime in September or October."

"Six months!"

"We will if we're lucky."

Jim whistled.

"How about it?" asked Tom. "Are you glad

now that you signed up for three years?"

"You know I am," was Jim's prompt reply.

All day the men on the keelboats struggled upstream against the rushing waters of the Mississippi. The annual spring floods made the journey dangerous and difficult.

Shortly before dark the land party was ordered to make camp. The horses and mules were hobbled and fed. The keelboats were anchored and the men went ashore. Campfires were started and supper cooked. General Ashley and Major Henry joined the men on shore for supper, but after they had eaten they returned to their boat.

The day's work was done. The men gathered around the campfires to sing and try to outdo each other in story-telling.

Jim and Tom were with a group of men at one of the campfires. Tom was laughing and talking. Jim was listening to the stories and thinking to himself how lucky he was to be on his way west.

Suddenly a man at the next campfire rose to his feet. He walked slowly toward Jim.

"Say, aren't you the kid I met in Old John's

gun shop early this morning?" he demanded.

Jim stood up and answered, "I am."

"What's your name?"

"Jim Bridger."

"So you're Jim Bridger. Well, well. Guess you have heard of me. I'm Wolf Andrews."

Jim nodded.

"Then you know that when I say I'll get even with someone I generally do."

"So I hear."

Wolf's eyes narrowed. "Trying to show me you're not afraid of me, kid?"

"Any one who bullies a feeble old man who can't defend himself is a coward," Jim replied looking straight at Wolf. "I'm not afraid of a coward and that's what I think you are."

"Me! I'm the best Indian fighter in the West."

"Then keep on fighting Indians."

"Why you—you greenhorn trapper trying to bluff me."

"I'm not bluffing," said Jim.

"Do you hear that?" sneered Wolf turning toward the men. They were silent. Wolf shrugged his shoulders and walked back to his campfire. Jim took his place in the circle again.

"Let me give you some advice, Jim," said a trapper. "Wolf is an old-timer and you're a greenhorn. Don't quarrel with him or as sure as you were born you'll have your hands full of trouble."

"Jim won't quarrel with him," said Tom quickly. "But if Wolf tries to start something I think Jim can finish it."

"You can't beat Wolf at his own game," spoke up another trapper. He shook his head. "I know because when I was a greenhorn I tried it." He turned to Jim. "Leave him alone, Jim, and you'll get along all right."

"I don't intend to quarrel with Wolf Andrews or any man in the outfit," replied Jim. "That isn't why I signed up to trap beaver. I'm out here to become as good a mountain man as you old-timers and," he paused, "to see the West."

---

1. Why did Jim want to go West?
2. Do you think Jim will become a good mountain man? Why?

Keelboats on the Missouri

CAMP was quiet early that evening. The men were tired after a hard day. Although they had traveled only twenty miles it had been a struggle against the swift current of the river all the way.

Some of the trappers went back to the boats to spend the night. Most of them, however, spread their blankets on the ground and fell asleep near the dying campfires.

Jim and Tom were tired, too, but they laughed and talked in low voices beside their campfire. They were joined by an old trapper.

"I'm looking for Jim Bridger," he said.

"I'm Jim Bridger."

The old trapper studied Jim for a minute. "I like your spirit," he said as he sat down beside Jim. "Any man who can stand up against Wolf Andrews will get along."

"Let's forget about him," said Jim. "I'd rather

15

talk about the West. You've been out there. Tell me about the country. What's it like and what about the Indians?"

"Well, the rivers and streams are full of beaver and there is an Indian behind every tree. I went out there the first time with Major Henry. That was thirteen years ago, back in 1809. We made Three Forks on the Missouri River, but the Blackfeet Indians drove us out in a hurry. Yes, sir, Henry is quite a man. He was the first American trader to take the fur trade across the Rocky Mountains and I was with him. He knows all there is to know about trapping and fighting Indians."

"Why did Major Henry choose General Ashley as a partner?" asked Tom. "The general isn't a trapper."

"That's true," laughed the old trapper. "Ashley doesn't know any more about trapping than a Mississippi steamboat captain. But his business ability and common sense will make up for his lack of experience. He is an honest man. His word is good. That counts in the West.

"Ashley loves the West," the old trapper continued. "At heart he is an explorer. And that is one reason why he will be a good leader. You see, boys, there is a lot more to this business than setting traps. You have to find new valleys, rivers, and streams, and then remember how to get back to them in a land where there are no roads. Ashley and Henry are a good team. One likes to explore and the other likes to trap. I certainly hope this new idea of theirs in trapping succeeds."

"New?" questioned Jim. "What's new about it?"

"Did you ever hear of a fur company taking a hundred men out to trap?"

"No, but many small parties go out each year."

"Sure, sure," the old trapper agreed. "Small parties of trappers and a few traders go out every year. The trappers bring their furs back to St. Louis and the traders buy most of their fur packs from the Indians. That's the way it has always been done. Now, of course, Ashley and Henry will buy all the furs they can from the Indians, but they will not depend upon the Indians. That's why they hired us."

"I understand," said Jim. "Our party of one hundred men will do the trapping."

"Right, and in one year we will have more fur packs than a small party can bring back in five years."

"Ashley and Henry should make a lot of money," said Tom. "I went out with a small party two years ago and we came back with twenty thousand dollars' worth of furs."

Jim whistled.

"You had a streak of luck," said the old trapper. "What did you do with your share of the money? I'll bet you spent every cent of it."

Tom shook his head. "No, I saved most of it."

The old trapper roared with laughter. "Saved most of it! You'll never be a mountain man, Tom. A real mountain man can't spend his money fast enough. What are you going to do with it?"

"Well, some day Ashley and Henry will retire from the fur business. More than likely they will sell this company to some of their trappers. I want to be one of the men who will buy it."

"If that is what you want I hope you get it."

"I've already decided on a good partner."

"Who?"

"Jim Bridger."

"Me!" exclaimed Jim. "I'm not going to be a business man and worry about the price of furs. I'm going to trap and see the country."

The old trapper rose to his feet. "Well, I think I'll get some sleep," he said. "If you fellows buy the Rocky Mountain Fur Company tonight be sure to let Ashley and Henry know about it. We're only twenty miles from St. Louis and they might want to go back if this company doesn't belong to them any longer."

He spread his blanket on the ground and wrapped himself in it. "Jim," he laughed, "don't let Tom's plans for your future upset you. You'll have time to enjoy yourself, and plenty of chance to see the country. He'll wait until you are 'up to beaver' before he makes you a partner."

"Up to beaver? What do you mean?"

"Tell him, Tom. I'm going to sleep."

"If a man is 'up to beaver,' Jim, it means that he is better than a good trapper," Tom explained.

"He is an expert. Trapping all animals is hard work. You have to know their habits so well that they can't fool you. You have to know how and where they live, what they eat, and how to follow their trails. You have to know, from one quick look at a footprint, what kind of animal made it and how long ago it was made. You have to tell at a glance whether the animal was running or walking and how big the animal is and how old. And of all animals the beaver is the hardest to trap. He is a smart rascal and it takes plenty of sense to get him in your trap."

"Does it take long to become an expert trapper?"

"You mean 'up to beaver?' " laughed Tom. "Lots of men have trapped for years and are good trappers but have never been 'up to beaver.' But there are men who make it in one season. Sometimes even these men are fooled by the beavers. Then instead of being 'up to beaver' they say the beaver is 'up to the trapper.' Come on," he added, "it's getting late. Let's roll in."

Before sunrise the sleeping men were awakened by the loud notes of a bugle. At once the camp came to life. Fires were started and as the men cooked breakfast they were given their orders for the day. In the hurry of breaking camp the laughter and story-telling of the night before were forgotten. This was a new day with hard work ahead and none of the precious daylight hours could be wasted.

Within an hour the men were on their way. Slowly the polers pushed the keelboats up the river. The mounted land party followed along the bank.

The land party was made up of two sections, one for each keelboat. As Jim and Tom had helped pole the first boat yesterday, they were now riding with the first section of the land party.

"Jim," said Tom as they rode along, "Wolf Andrews was looking for you before we left camp. Did you see him?"

"Yes," answered Jim. "He seems to think that if he tells me often enough that he's a good Indian fighter, I'll forget how he treated Old John."

"If Wolf makes any trouble for you, you can count on me to help."

"I know I can depend upon you for help, Tom. But I must make my own way in the West. No one can do it for me, not even you, and you are my best friend."

"You're right, Jim."

They rode on in silence watching their boat in the river.   The party was nearing the mouth

of the Missouri River. The polers were making slow progress because the water was getting deeper.

"When we start up the Missouri," said Jim, "I'll know we're really on our way."

Tom grinned, "You'll know it before then because we'll soon be pulling the boat. The current is getting too swift. The polers won't be able to make any headway so we'll have to take over and tow the boat."

"How many miles will we make today?"

"As long as the river remains at flood stage we should make about twenty miles a day," answered Tom. "But before the summer is over we'll be lucky if we make five miles on some days."

"Is that another trapper's yarn?"

"No," laughed Tom, "you'll know I'm telling the truth when we spend a few hours trying to tow a boat off a sand bar or a snag."

Just then a call came from the leading keelboat. The long cordelle, or towing rope, fastened to the high mast on the boat, was brought ashore. Amid cheers and shouts the first section of the land party went into action.

The men raced their horses into position. They formed in single file along the bank of the river. The last rider grabbed the cordelle and passed it along to the rider in front of him. The cordelle was more than a thousand feet long. Each man tied a short rope from his saddle to the cordelle.

When they were ready the leading rider gave the signal. The men pushed their feet into their stirrups and leaned forward in their saddles.

"All together!"

The horses plunged forward. The cordelle straightened out like a steel rope from the boat to the shore. The boat did not move and the sudden shock jerked the horses to a dead stop. Men were thrown to the ground. Horses slipped on the wet bank and fell with their riders into the river. Men shouted to one another as they tried to hold the half-wild horses.

The commands of the leading rider finally brought order. The men were again in position and the signal was repeated. Again the riders were jerked to a sudden stop.

Three times—four times the riders charged forward. But they were unable to move the boat.

"Have your men pull toward the left," the captain shouted to the leader of the land party.

"I'll tell them what to do," the leader replied. "This isn't the first boat I've towed up the Missouri."

"The Missouri!" Jim shouted. His heart leaped for now the West was before him. The muddy, yellow waters of the Missouri had come from the snowcapped peaks of the Rocky Mountains.

At last the boat was pulled off the sand bar.

Slowly the land party towed the boat up the first mile of the Missouri. Then the polers took over again. They had gone only a short distance, however, when the keelboat hit a snag.

Again the cordelle was brought ashore and the land party formed their line.

One hour—two hours passed and then at last the men cheered. The boat was moving. Slowly the land party towed it to deeper water. The delay was over and once again Ashley's men were on their way.

The land party towed the boats most of the day. The men guided their horses over the path close to the bank of the river. At times the bank was too narrow and slippery for the horses. The men dismounted and, throwing the cordelle over their shoulders, pulled the boat by hand. In places where the bank was covered with trees and shrubs a path had to be cut before they could proceed. If the leader decided it would take too long to cut a trail he ordered the men to swim with their horses across the river to the opposite bank. Then as quickly as they could the men reformed their long, single file and struggled on.

Late in the afternoon it began to rain. Lightning flashed across the dull gray April sky. Sharp claps of thunder rose above the roar of the rushing waters. But the men pushed on through the downpour until Ashley ordered a halt.

Camp was made. The men ate a supper of cold meat as there was no dry wood for fires. That night they slept in wet clothing.

"Well, Jim, this is the life of a mountain man," said Tom. "What do you think of it?"

Jim laughed, but instead of answering he asked, "We're on our way to the West, aren't we?"

"That's right."

"Well, then I like it," answered Jim. "I don't care how long it takes or how hard I have to work. I'm headed the right way. I'm headed for the land of the beaver."

The Midnight Watch

ASHLEY'S MEN had been on their way less than two weeks when they met with their first serious accident. The leading keelboat hit a snag in the river and sank so quickly that the men on board narrowly escaped with their lives. The loss of the boat was a great blow as it was loaded with ten thousand dollars' worth of trapping supplies. Like true Westerners, however, Ashley and Henry did not let the accident discourage them. They ordered the men to push on.

Day after day, week after week the fur trappers traveled on up the Missouri River. Spring with its bright flowers and sudden rains gave way to the blazing heat of the summer months.

Every day, from sunrise to sunset, the men faced the back-breaking job of fighting their way upstream. Every day it was the same old story of countless delays caused by sand bars and snags.

Time and again the polers were unable to pole the boat and each time the land party was called into action. And always it was the same old story of more accidents and spills. The half-wild horses and stubborn mules bucked and reared, tying the cordelle into a hopeless knot of kicking animals and shouting men.

Again and again the men swam across the river hoping to follow an easier path along the opposite bank. Often it was worse. Then they walked the long weary miles as they pulled the boat with the cordelle cutting into their shoulders.

And day after day, day after day the trip was the same. They seldom made over twenty miles a day. Most of the time they made less. But mile after mile they struggled on. Slipping and falling and rising to slip and fall again, they pushed on ever closer to the land of the beaver.

The old experienced trappers did not mind the slow progress of the party. They knew the accidents and delays could not be avoided. The young greenhorns, however, were restless. They did not complain about the hard work. They were used to it. But the deadly sameness of the days made them quarrelsome and quick-tempered. More than anything else they hated the snail-like pace of each day's march.

All but one—young Jim Bridger.

To Jim each day was one of high adventure. To him the trip up the river was not a slow, uninteresting journey. It was wonderful. Everything was different and it was ever changing. The old familiar woodland country gave way to the vast rolling plains. Like a great green sea of tall grass the plains stretched on ahead for endless miles.

It was all new country to Jim. But the millions of buffalo which roamed the rich pasture land, and the deer, the elk, the antelope, the wild game birds, the wolves, and the rattlesnakes knew its every secret. And this was the homeland and hunting grounds of the proud, bold Plains Indians.

"What more could anyone want?" Jim often asked himself. "Isn't this enough?"

And for him it was more than enough. He was always good-natured. No job in camp or on the march was too difficult. He obeyed every order quickly and did his work with a ready smile.

"That Bridger kid takes to this life like one of us," an old trapper said one night to a group of men gathered around a campfire. "I never saw anyone like him. He's the last one to turn in at night and yet in the morning he's always the first one up and ready to go."

"He works like a beaver all day, too," said another trapper. "I like him."

"I think he'll be one of the first greenhorns 'up to beaver,' " said Tom.

"I don't see how he could fail to be," laughed a man. "He asks enough questions."

"I'm waiting to see how he acts in an Indian fight," spoke up Wolf Andrews. "A man isn't worth his salt unless he's a good Indian fighter."

"Give him a chance," defended Tom, "and he may become a better Indian fighter than you are. He has already proved to be a better worker."

Wolf sneered. "Ashley didn't hire me to work. He hired me because I'm the best Indian fighter he could get. And I—"

"Ashley and Henry expect every man to do his

share of work," broke in a trapper. "And now that we are on the plains, you will have to do your share like the rest of us."

Jim joined the men. He glanced about and walked straight to Wolf Andrews.

"Andrews," he said, "you are to be one of the guards tonight."

"Oh, yes? Who said so?"

"Major Henry."

"Tell him to get another guard."

Major Henry's sharp voice brought all the men to their feet. "Wolf," he said as he strode forward, "you can tell me yourself."

"Major, I would just as soon stand guard tonight," said Wolf, "but we are now in Indian territory and I should get my sleep at night. You never can tell what will happen when the Pawnees and Sioux find out we are here."

"They have known it for some time," replied Major Henry, "and that's why for the past week we have posted a double guard. Each man has his turn, and now—tonight, from twelve to two—it's your turn."

"You can't expect me to stand guard, Major."

"I expect every man to take his turn."

"Yes, I know, but I'm an Indian fighter."

"I'm an Indian fighter, too, and I'm also in command of this party," snapped Henry. "You have your orders. Report to Bruce Bastian. He's in charge of the guard tonight." Without another word Henry walked away.

Wolf turned to Jim. "Who else is on guard?"

"Bill Sublette and myself."

"You!" Wolf's eyes narrowed. "You would be one of them!" He spat in the fire.

"Turn in, Wolf," said a trapper, anxious to avoid a quarrel between the Indian fighter and young Jim.

"I'll turn in when I get ready," Wolf growled. But he left the men and disappeared into the darkness. He was gone from camp for some time. When he returned he spread a blanket on the ground and went to sleep.

"Why was he out of camp so long?" Tom nodded toward the sleeping Andrews.

Jim shrugged his shoulders.

"Here comes Bastian," said Tom. "He's probably looking for you. Bruce," he called, "are you looking for Jim?"

"Yes, where is he?"

"He's here with me."

Bastian, an experienced trapper with flashing brown eyes and black curly hair, dressed in fringed buckskin, came quickly to the campfire. He sat down beside Jim. "I'm in charge of the guard tonight," he said, "and I don't want to lose any of the horses or mules on my watch. I want you and that other greenhorn, Bill Sublette, to keep your eyes and ears open. Do you understand?"

"I do," answered Jim.

"Good. This is the first time you have been on guard duty with me, and this is Indian country."

"Don't worry about Jim," said Tom. "You can count on him and you can count on Bill Sublette, too."

"Well, we can't be too careful. You know these Plains Indians." Bastian shook his head. "They would rather steal horses than eat. If we can't keep our horses now we will certainly lose all of them when we finally reach the Crow country."

"Are the Crows better at stealing horses than the Sioux and the Pawnees?" asked Jim.

Bastian slapped Jim on the shoulder. "They are all good at it, but the Crows are experts. Most Indians just try to steal as many horses as they can, but a Crow will spot the horse he wants. No matter if that horse is within two feet of a guard, the Crow will get the horse and the guard won't hear one sound." He laughed, "Tom, you know what we old trappers say about them."

Tom grinned, "Yes, and it's almost true. We say, 'Look away for a minute and a Crow can steal the horse you are riding.' "

"They must be good if you old fur trappers admit it," said Jim.

"Get some sleep, Jim," said Bastian rising to his feet. "I'll call you in plenty of time."

At midnight the four men took over their guard duties. As Jim reported to the guard he was to relieve, the man said, "Keep your eyes and ears open, son. Remember we can make the trip without you, but we need our horses and mules."

Jim made no reply. He knew how important the horses and mules were to the fur trappers.

The loss of only one horse or mule was serious, but the loss of even as few as ten or twelve was a disaster. In the wilderness the fur trappers depended almost entirely upon their pack animals for transportation. Many trapping leaders placed the safety of their animals above the lives of their men.

Ashley and Henry, however, did not value their animals more than the lives of their men. But they did demand that the men be ever watchful and alert.

"Who else is on Bastian's watch?" asked the guard.

"Bill Sublette and Wolf Andrews."

The man laughed. "So Wolf had to take his turn. Where did Bastian station him?"

"On the north side facing the plains."

"Well, don't let an Indian get your hair tonight," the man said starting back to the nearby camp.

Gun in hand, Jim stood quietly in the moonlight for a few minutes. He listened intently to become used to the sounds of the night. His eyes studied every dark shadow around him. The stillness was broken by the soft neighing of the hobbled horses as they moved about, or as they stamped their feet. Now and then an owl hooted and far to the right a wolf howled and was answered by another wolf far to the left.

Quickly and without making a sound Jim walked along his side of the camp. He peered into the darkness which covered the open plains and wondered what adventures were waiting there for him. The sound of footsteps made him halt.

"That you, Bridger?" came Wolf's voice from the darkness.

"Yes."

"Well, you don't need to come around here. I'll take care of this side of the camp and I don't need any help from you."

"My line of guard duty comes to this point."

"Do as I tell you!" ordered Wolf Andrews.

"Bastian gave me my orders," replied Jim.

Jim did not meet Wolf as he made his next three rounds.

"I wonder where he is?" Jim asked himself.

Quietly he started down Wolf's side of the camp. He had gone only a short distance when suddenly he stopped. Ahead were two men. They were talking in low, but excited voices.

"No, not tonight. Go!" said one of the men. It was Wolf's voice.

The other man said something which Jim could not hear.

"No, no, go!" said Wolf again.

"Andrews," called Jim, "are you in trouble?"

There was no answer.

Jim ran forward.

"Stay where you are," snapped Wolf as he hurried toward Jim. The other man turned and fled. His footsteps made only the faintest of sounds.

"Who was that?" asked Jim.

"None of your business."

"Was it one of our men from camp?"

Wolf hesitated for a second. "Yes," he answered. "Yes, that's who it was. One of the men from camp. Now get back to your station."

Jim returned to his side of the camp. He kept

thinking of the soft footsteps of the running man. "That wasn't a white man," he said to himself. "Only an Indian could run that quietly."

Jim reported what had happened to Bastian. "I tell you I'm sure it was an Indian," said Jim.

"Thanks, Jim. I'll look into this."

When Bastian questioned Andrews, the Indian fighter sneered, "That Bridger kid is trying to make trouble for me. I was talking to a man from camp. I'll take you to him."

At two o'clock Bastian and his men were relieved by four other guards and they returned to camp. They followed Wolf as he led them to a man sleeping on the ground a little apart from the other trappers.

"Tell Bastian that you came out and talked to me while I was on guard duty," said Wolf, kicking the man with the toe of his moccasin.

"What? What?" the man sat up rubbing his eyes. "Oh, yes, I did," he added quickly.

Bastian turned to Jim.

"I guess I was wrong," said Jim.

But as Jim walked away he said to Bill Sublette,

"I still think he was talking to an Indian."

"They seemed to be telling the truth," said Bill.
"If I were you I would forget it."

But Jim couldn't forget. At the first break of
day he hurried to the spot where Wolf and the man
had been talking. He looked for their footprints,
but they were not easy to find in the early light.
He dropped to his knees and crawled along the
ground. Suddenly he reached for something in
the grass.

Later that morning when Wolf Andrews awakened, Jim was waiting for him.

"Last night your friend left something," said
Jim. "You might want to give it back to him."

"Why, you—" Andrews sprang to his feet.

Jim was holding in his hand an eagle feather
—a feather worn by an Indian brave.

---

1. How did most of the fur traders and trappers get
their fur packs?

2. What was Ashley and Henry's new plan?

3. What does "up to beaver" mean?

4. Would you rather ride with the land party or work
with the polers on the keelboats?

Trailed by Indians

WOLF ANDREWS' fist caught Jim under the chin and sent him reeling to the ground. Jim was stunned by the blow. In the mist before his eyes the Indian fighter appeared like a giant, cruel and evil. Everything in camp whirled about him. And floating slowly earthward, the eagle feather spun round and round.

Wolf saw the feather, too. He grabbed at it, but missed and the feather fell to the ground. He leaned over, picked it up and stuck it into the front of his buckskin shirt. Then with a savage growl he plunged toward Jim.

It had taken Wolf only a few seconds to pick up the feather, but that was all the time Jim needed. He was on his feet and ready. He blocked Wolf's blow, and swung with all his might.

"Wolf! Jim!" a trapper shouted. "Stop it!"

They paid no attention, nor did they stop

fighting until they were separated. Even then, Jim held by Bill Sublette and Bastian, struggled to free himself, as two trappers led Wolf away.

During the fight General Ashley had joined the men. In the excitement they had not noticed him.

"Bridger," he said stepping forward, "if you can't get along with Wolf Andrews, then stay away from him."

"I must tell you what happened," said Jim.

"I don't listen to the quarrels of my men."

"But, General, I must tell you."

"I don't listen to the quarrels of my men," Ashley repeated. He turned and hurried toward the river.

Jim watched the general for a minute. Then he walked slowly to the campfire where Tom and a group of men were cooking breakfast.

"Come on, Jim," called Tom. "You're leaving camp with me in ten minutes. Have your gun and plenty of ammunition."

"My gun and plenty of ammunition?"

"Yes, Henry has put me in charge of a new hunting party," explained Tom. "I'm taking you and

Bill Sublette with me. I'll meet you here."

Jim whistled. "Thanks, Tom. Thanks a lot."

A short time later the three hunters mounted their horses and left camp. They rode northward across the plains.

They had gone only a mile when Tom slowed his horse to a trot. He pointed to a spot ahead where the tall grass was tramped down. It was clear that horses had been hobbled there, and that Indians had camped near by.

"Bill, ride back to Major Henry," ordered Tom. "Tell him to warn the men that we have found a deserted Indian camp. Tell him to send the scouts on here with you. They can follow the Indians' trail."

Bill turned his horse about and raced away.

"Let's look around while we wait for Bill," said Tom. "This camp may have been used by peaceful braves, but," he added, "we can't be too careful."

"I think the braves are trailing our party. Maybe they are waiting to steal our horses."

"What makes you think so?"

Jim told Tom about the midnight watch and

about his fight with Wolf. "And now I'm more suspicious of Wolf than ever," said Jim.

"I don't like it." Tom shook his head. "Jim, you and I are going to watch him. If he is up to something we can find out what it is."

A short time later Bill returned with the scouts. As Tom pointed out the Indian trail he said, "From the signs I would say there are about twenty braves in the party."

"Probably a small hunting party," said a scout.

"You mean a hunting party of twenty horse thieves," spoke up another.

"That's what we want to find out," laughed the leader. "Come on, boys, let's ride."

The scouts raced away. The hunters turned their horses northward. Early in the afternoon they sighted a herd of more than a thousand buffalo.

Tom explained that they must approach the herd against the wind for the buffalo had a keen sense of smell. If they rode in with the wind the buffalo would smell them and stampede. He told them how to shoot the great shaggy beasts.

"The bullet," he said, "must be aimed directly

into the heart region. Now the way to do it is to
ride close to the animal and aim carefully just behind the left shoulder. Take your time and don't
get excited. Don't fire until your aim is true. Come
on, boys, follow me."

They raced their horses along the edge of the
herd. Three rifles barked and three buffalo dropped
in their tracks. The herd, frightened by the gun-
fire, broke into a stampede.

The hunters watched the headlong flight of the
herd until it disappeared. Then, laughing and jok-
ing, they began to butcher the buffalo they had
killed. When they had finished they started back
to join their outfit on the Missouri River.

When they reached the river they met the scouts.
The scouts had followed the trail from the deserted
Indian camp and had finally located the braves.

"They claim to be out on a hunt," said the scout
leader.

"Have you reported to Major Henry?" asked
Tom.

"Yes, I have," answered the leader. "He thinks
the band is following our party. He has ordered

us to keep even closer watch from now on."

"How did you get along today, Tom?" a scout asked.

"Fine," laughed Tom. "I'll make hunters out of these greenhorns yet."

Early each morning the hunters left camp. Jim and Bill had much to learn about hunting on the plains. Fortunately for them, Tom was a good teacher as well as a good hunter. He taught them how to follow trails, read signs, and to use signals.

It was a real job to kill enough game every day to feed a hundred hungry men. The teamwork of the hunters, however, made it easier. When one sighted a herd of buffalo, he signaled the others. The three guided their horses to the rear of the herd. When they were ready Tom gave the signal. They raced into position and three rifles barked.

When they hunted elk or deer they usually rode along the high, wooded bluffs of the river. As soon as they spotted a herd they slipped from their saddles and hobbled their horses. Then quietly they stalked forward until they were within rifle range.

One afternoon as the hunters were on their way

back to the river Jim sighted a band of twenty Indians in the distance. Although some of the braves were mounted on Indian ponies, most of them were riding good horses. The hunters paid little attention to the horses as they knew the horse-stealing ability of the Indians. Even the snow-white horse of the chief did not seem important.

When the hunters sighted the same band the following two days, however, they were disturbed. There was no mistaking the spirited snow-white horse of the chief.

As soon as they reached camp the hunters reported to Major Henry. "I'm sure those Indians are up to something," said Tom.

"Why don't we fight them?" asked Bill.

"Indians seldom attack an alert party," replied Henry. "They depend almost entirely on surprise. Anyway we're not out here to fight Indians, Bill. We're here for just one purpose—to trap beaver."

"Couldn't the Indians be waiting for a war party to join them?" asked Jim.

"Yes, they could be, Jim. But that is the chance we must take. This is more than a question of

defeating twenty braves. We are in enemy territory and we are surrounded by thousands of hostile
Indians. I have fought the Indians many times,
but I have never started a fight. We shall try to
avoid trouble this time, but if we are attacked we
will fight."

Henry turned to Tom. "Keep watching those Indians," he ordered. "Report to me each night."

Every day during the next week the hunters
spotted the band of Indians. As always, the chief
on the snow-white horse was with them. When the
hunters tried to talk with them the Indians raced
away.

"They would like to make trouble for us all
right," said Tom one day as the three hunters
watched the last of the band disappear over the
top of a hill.

"And I still think Wolf Andrews has something
to do with it," said Jim. "Don't you, Tom?"

"Yes, I do," answered Tom, "but the horses are
guarded all the time. The Indians may get tired
of trailing the outfit. Then, too, I think Wolf knows
that we are watching him."

"He ought to know it by this time," laughed Jim. "He is the first person I look for every night, and it isn't because I'm fond of him either."

In April, when the trapping party left St. Louis, the young greenhorns expected to fight one Indian battle after another. They were disappointed that the party had reached the territory of what is now the state of North Dakota without a fight.

For awhile it seemed that the band of Indians led by the chief riding the snow-white horse might cause trouble. But now even the excitement of being trailed was gone. For the past week neither the scouts nor the hunters had seen the band of braves.

Late one afternoon in August the hunters were on their way back to join their party. As they rode along Tom said, "I wish we had spotted that band of redskins today."

"I thought you were glad they weren't trailing us," said Bill. "What are you worrying about now?"

Tom laughed a little. "Now I'm worried because we don't see them."

"I'm worried, too," said Jim. "I don't know why, but I just feel that something is wrong."

They rode on in silence. They let their horses follow the trail at a slow pace. The trail led them across the open country to a bluff overlooking the river.

About a mile downstream the approaching party could be seen. Along the west bank came the land party and the guards with the extra mules and horses. The keelboat was far out in the river.

"Well, there's our outfit," said Jim, "and I'm surely glad to see it."

"Let's ride down to meet the men," said Bill.

"That's a good idea." Tom headed his horse to a path which zigzagged down the bluff to the flat river bottom. "Follow me."

They made their way down the path and left the game they had shot during the day under a tall tree. Then, laughing and talking, they started downstream.

Suddenly Jim reined in his horse. "Indians!" he pointed. "Indians!"

Out of the west a band of screaming Indians

galloped down the bluff just ahead of the land party. At a signal from the leading brave, the Indians reined in their horses and stopped. The brave rode forward to meet the trappers.

"Come on, boys," called Tom. "If this means trouble we want to be with our men."

They touched their horses lightly and raced to join their fellow trappers.

"Isn't that Wolf Andrews talking to the brave?" asked Tom as he slowed his horse down to a trot.

"Yes, it is," Jim answered.

"Let's find out what this is all about."

As they neared the two men they heard Wolf say, "Tell your chief that I am not afraid of his threats. Tell him to stop trailing us or we will fight."

"We no want to fight," replied the brave. "I tell you that before. We want guns. You promise guns long time now."

"I said to stop trailing this outfit."

"You trick us." The brave waved his tomahawk in Wolf's face. "Give us guns or we take horses."

"Andrews!" called Tom, "do you need our help?"

"No," snapped Wolf. He whirled his horse

around. "Get over there with the men. I can settle this."

"Let Major Henry settle it," suggested Tom. "He is in command."

"He's on the boat so I'm in command right now. I'll handle this my own way."

"Do you know this Indian?"

"I never saw him in my life."

"You lie! You lie!" screamed the brave. "I talk to you before."

"I never saw you in my life," Wolf shouted. "Now take your braves and get out of here."

Without another word the brave headed back to the waiting Indians. Wolf kicked his horse and rode toward the land party. The hunters followed him.

The Indians shouted a war whoop. At the signal a war party of almost two hundred braves swept down the bluff. The chief, in full war dress, was in the lead. He was mounted on the handsome snow-white horse.

The attack was on. Arrows whizzed through the air.

"Get ready, men," called Wolf. He gave the order. "Fire!"

The guns of the trappers blazed.

The greenhorns were stunned by the swiftness of the attack. They were untrained and reckless. They had yet to learn the strictest law of the mountain men—to fight together. But as they recovered from their shock, they fought bravely to defend themselves and the prized horses and mules.

The Indians retreated. While they were preparing for another attack Wolf ordered the old-timers to take over the front line of defense. Jim, Bill, and a few other plucky greenhorns were with them.

Jim forgot his suspicion and distrust of Wolf. Now, in spite of himself, he admired the cool courage of the Indian fighter.

The Indians attacked again. The steady fire from the front line threw them back. But they returned. This time they circled and surrounded the trappers.

"Here's my chance to get that chief," shouted Wolf. He fired. The chief pitched forward and fell to the ground, dead. The white horse reared into the air as a wild shot hit him. The horse stumbled and fell beside his master and lay still.

When the braves saw their chief fall, they attacked with renewed fury. Slowly they gained ground.

The last attack was over in less than fifteen minutes. The Indians were gone and with them every horse and mule in the outfit. Five trappers had been killed and twenty had been wounded.

"Well, Jim," said Tom, "now we will never be able to prove that Wolf was mixed up with that band of Indians. The brave he was talking to and the chief were both killed."

"Yes," replied Jim, "and so was the trapper Wolf claimed was with him that night on guard duty."

They were interrupted as Wolf joined them. "Ashley and Henry are coming ashore," he said. "They will question us about the attack. What are you going to tell them?"

"The truth," Jim and Tom answered quickly.

"Go ahead. It's your word against mine."

As the Indian fighter walked away Tom said,

"He's right, Jim. They won't believe our story."

"Why not?"

"Because his clever lies will make the truth sound ridiculous."

"Well, then I guess he wins this time."

"Yes, he wins this time," agreed Tom.

That night quiet groups of discouraged men sat around the campfires. None of them spoke. They just sat there staring into the dancing flames.

"Men," came the voice of Major Henry, "General Ashley and I want to talk to you."

When the men gathered around the two leaders Ashley said, "I do not need to tell you that our defeat is serious. You know it. But we are not turning back. We are going on."

The men cheered.

Major Henry raised his hand for silence. "We can't get to Three Forks this fall," he said. "But we'll push on to the Yellowstone River two hundred miles from here. We will fort up there for the winter. General Ashley and some men will return to St. Louis to equip another trapping party. They will meet us next fall on the Yellowstone.

"This coming spring the rest of us will head for Three Forks, the land of the beaver, and—" he paused, "the land of the Blackfeet Indians. The Blackfeet are the fiercest tribe of Indians I have ever met. They are powerful enemies and they are determined to keep us out of their country.

"Now, you greenhorns have just been through your first Indian attack. Those of you who think it was a real Indian fight should return to St. Louis with General Ashley. Why, those horse-thieving Indians are like squaws compared to the bloody Blackfeet! I want only the men who can take plenty of action to remain with me. If you want to fall out now, raise your hands."

Not a man moved.

"Then it's settled," smiled the major. "I can't promise that you will all become good trappers— 'up to beaver.' But I can promise that you will have a chance to prove your worth as mountain men."

———————

1. Why didn't Henry attack the Indians?
2. What did the greenhorns have to learn about fighting?
3. Give your definition of teamwork.

"Up to Beaver"

THE TRAPPERS finally reached the Yellowstone River late in September. General Ashley and a small party of men, including Wolf Andrews and Bill Sublette, soon left on the return trip to St. Louis.

Henry and the rest of the men set to work to fort up for the winter. They built several log cabins for themselves and a strong corral for the horses they hoped to buy from the Indians. They made a high stockade of sharpened poles to enclose the buildings. The men named the little post "Fort Henry" in honor of their well-liked leader.

When the fort was completed the men visited the nearby Indian villages and bought many horses from the braves. The trappers explored the surrounding country and went on hunting trips.

Frequently the Indians came to the fort. Sometimes they made camp near by and remained several days. Major Henry was always courteous, but he was ever on the alert. He kept his men on constant guard duty. He encouraged the greenhorns to spend as much time as they could with the Indians. He warned them, however, not to trust the braves of even the friendly tribes.

This was young Jim Bridger's first chance to learn all he could about the Indians, and he made the most of it. When his work was finished he hurried to an Indian camp. He made friends with the braves, and in a short time he was their favorite trapper.

Jim's first attempts to talk to the braves of the different tribes made the Indians howl with laughter. When they saw that he really wanted to learn, however, they helped him. They spent hours teaching him not only their tribal language but the sign language used by all the Plains Indians.

Jim's best friend was Tall Bear, the son of a Sioux war chief. Slim and straight as a bright-feathered arrow, he was already looked upon by the people of his tribe as their next war chief.

Tall Bear was proud and haughty. He seldom

spoke to any white man, but when he was with Jim he laughed and talked. They had good times together.

One day while they were out hunting Tall Bear said to Jim, "You like my people. I can tell. You talk like friend. I trust you."

"I hope we can always be friends," replied Jim, remembering Henry's warning not to trust even the friendly braves.

"We break camp tomorrow," said Tall Bear. "We go back to Sioux country."

"Some day we will meet again," said Jim.

Tall Bear nodded. "We meet again some day."

The winter on the Yellowstone was long and cold. Howling blizzards from the northwest swept across the country and often sent the temperature tumbling down to fifty degrees below zero. Ice blocked the rivers and streams. Snowstorms raged and the snow covered the earth like a great white blanket.

All winter the men were busy, especially the greenhorns. Major Henry saw to that. He organized them into groups and changed them from one job to another so that they would learn how to do every job in camp. They learned to cook, to make and mend their equipment, to mold bullets, and to sew their own buckskin clothes. Some trappers stood guard and tended the horses while others hunted and scouted.

At last the first signs of spring came to the beautiful Yellowstone country. The trapping season was on and the trappers were ready. Leaving a few men to guard the fort and supplies, Major Henry and the rest of the men started up the Missouri River. They were headed for the rich beaver streams around Three Forks. Jim was one of the young greenhorns included in the trapping party.

Day after day the men pushed on. This was Indian territory, and the men were alert. Scouts rode on ahead keeping a sharp lookout for hostile Indians. Guards rode with the pack horses carrying the supplies needed for the trip. In camp each night double guards were always on duty. Every man slept with his rifle beside him.

The party was still many miles from Three Forks, but already beaver signs were becoming

more and more plentiful. Major Henry decided it
was time to begin trapping and the men agreed
with him.

Camp was made early that afternoon. The pack
horses were unloaded and turned out to graze
under the watchful eyes of their guards. The big
leather sacks of beaver traps were unpacked. Each
man was given six or eight traps. He was to use
them for the entire season. Henry kept a record
in the company's books of the traps given each man.

Although some of the old-timers preferred to
trap alone most of them chose partners. An experienced trapper usually picked the greenhorn he
thought would be one of the first "up to beaver."

When Major Henry handed six traps to Jim he
asked, "Who picked you for a partner, Jim?"

"Tom Fitzpatrick."

The major laughed, "If you aren't 'up to beaver'
it will be your own fault, not Tom's."

"I know it," grinned Jim.

"Here, take Tom's traps to him. I'm giving him
eight. Good luck to you, Jim."

Jim took the traps and hurried away. He looked

about and saw Tom talking to Bruce Bastian.

As Jim joined them Bruce said, "I was telling Tom that I wanted you for my partner and so did several of the old-timers."

"Thanks, Bastian," said Jim, "but Tom and I decided long ago that we would trap together. But if I'm not 'up to beaver' he may change his mind. Maybe then—"

"Oh no," broke in Bastian with a laugh. "If you aren't 'up to beaver' after trapping with Tom, I certainly don't want you as a partner."

"Jim won't have any trouble," spoke up Tom. "I'm giving him some of my bait to use until he makes his own and you know my bait is the best."

"It is good," admitted Bastian. "In fact it's almost as good as mine."

Castor, the bait used in trapping beaver, was the liquid from two small glands found in the beaver's body. A stick dipped into the castor was placed just above the trap. Unable to resist the strong scent of the bait the beaver was drawn to the spot. As he reached for the stick the steel jaws of the hidden trap snapped shut.

Each trapper made his own bait by adding a secret mixture to the castor. He loudly boasted that his bait was best. To question a trapper about his secret mixture was almost as great an offense as to be caught sleeping on guard duty. Only the greenest of greenhorns ever asked a mountain man what his secret was and he never asked but once.

"You're all alike," laughed Jim. "Every trapper claims his bait is the best. But you wait until I make mine. Now I really have a secret. An old Indian chief told me what to use."

Laughing and talking, Jim and Tom loaded their traps onto their horses and left the camp. They rode northward. The clinking of the traps was like music to Jim's ears. They came to a small stream and followed it looking for beaver signs.

"There are some signs around here," said Tom, "but not enough to suit me."

"We have time to find another stream," said Jim. "It's still an hour before sunset."

"Yes, and the best time to set our traps is after sunset anyway," said Tom. "Come on."

They rode on until they came to a place in the

woods where a number of trees had been cut down and carried away. It looked as if it had been done by expert woodsmen. But one quick glance was proof that it was the work of many beavers. The stumps were pointed and all about the same height. On each stump were the telltale broad tooth marks of the busy beaver. Piles of chips were scattered about showing where the beavers had gnawed the trees into shorter lengths to take down to the nearby stream. The path over which they had dragged the logs to the stream was cut with ruts.

"There's a beaver dam here all right," said Tom, "and that means a beaver colony. Come on."

They hobbled their horses and ran down to the stream. "There it is," said Tom pointing to the dam.

"Take a look at the beaver lodges," grinned Jim. "There must be a dozen or more of them."

The beavers had built their dam where a tree had fallen into the stream. They used the tree as a foundation. Against it they had piled logs, stones, and branches of all sizes and in every direction. The tangled mass was held together by a plaster of mud. The lodges, too, were made of logs, sticks, and branches.

"The lodges look like big and little brush piles," said Jim.

"They do," agreed Tom. "They don't look well built but they are. They are covered with a heavy plaster of mud which is many inches thick. The thick plaster helps keep the lodges warm and it's also fine protection from wild animals. I once saw a bear trying to tear a lodge apart, but with all his strength he could not do it."

"The beavers are smart little fellows."

"Smart!" exclaimed Tom. "Why, I have seen the rascals do things that are almost human. I remember once when I found all my traps had been snapped shut with sticks. I thought some trapper had played a joke on me. But, no sir, it was a couple of old beavers."

"How do you know?"

"I set my traps again in the same places and waited. After hours of waiting those two old beavers came swimming along with sticks in their mouths. What did they do?" Tom shook his head.

"Well, just as nice as you please, they swam over to my first trap. One beaver put a stick in the trap and it snapped shut. You may not believe me, Jim, but the sly old rascals winked at each other before they swam on to my next trap."

"What did you do?" laughed Jim.

"Do? What could I do? I was no longer 'up to beaver.' The beaver were up to me. I took my traps and went on to another stream."

Tom studied the dam, the lodges, and the stream. His keen eyes took in every detail. "We're in luck, Jim," he said. "This is where we set our traps."

They hurried to get their traps. As they came back through the woods, Tom asked, "Do you have your castor, Jim?"

Jim touched the pocket of his buckskin shirt. "The bottle is right here."

"We need some bait sticks," said Tom, "and some long poles to fasten to the chains on our traps. We can get them here. We must not walk around the stream any more than necessary. If we move about too much the beaver will smell our tracks and that will be the end of our trapping."

At sunset they were ready. They hurried back
to the little creek.

Jim waded out into the stream. Tom followed.
Jim shivered for the water was freezing cold. But
in his excitement he soon forgot it. He was about
to set his first beaver trap and that was all that
mattered. They waded upstream searching for

the runways, or slides, used by the beaver when they went ashore.

"There's one!" Jim almost shouted. "There on the left bank."

Tom nodded. "All right, Jim. Now remember there are three important things to do in setting a beaver trap."

"I remember," replied Jim. "The trap must be the right distance from the bank and it must be washed carefully so that it won't smell of human hands. The bait stick must be placed just above the trap."

"That's right. Now go ahead." Tom slapped Jim on the shoulder. "Good luck, old fellow."

To set a beaver trap was a tricky job, and Jim took his time to do it correctly. He examined the trap carefully. It was a good steel trap weighing about five pounds. The spring was strong and the jaws worked easily. He tested the five-foot chain to see that it was securely fastened to the trap. He tied a long leather cord to the trap. On the end of the cord was a float, or marker.

Jim waded close to the bank. For a minute or two he stood still looking in the muddy water for the bottom of the beaver slide. He found it and with the toe of his moccasin, dug a hole directly in the middle of the slide where the water was about four inches deep. The shallow hole would hold his trap in place. He washed the trap carefully in the icy water. Tom, watching him, laughed as Jim jokingly smelled the trap and washed it over and over again. He opened the steel jaws and carefully placed the set trap in the hole.

He ran a long pole through the ring at the end of the five-foot chain. He placed the pole farther out in the stream and pushed it into the muddy bottom to anchor it securely.

"Now for the bait," he said, pulling a stick and the bottle of castor from his pocket. He removed the cork from the horn bottle and dipped the stick into the strong-smelling bait. Holding the stick in one hand, he put the cork back in the bottle and slipped it into his pocket.

He leaned forward and stuck the bait stick over the trap. It was within easy reach of the beaver he hoped to find in his trap the next morning.

Laughing, Jim waded back to Tom.

"You did a good job," said Tom. He pointed to the marker floating on the water near the bait stick. "Now when a trapper tells you that you can 'float your stick' with his, you will know what he means. He rates you as an equal."

They made their way upstream to another beaver slide. Tom stayed with Jim until he had set two more traps. Tom was satisfied that Jim did not need any more help so he went on alone to set his own traps a little farther upstream.

It was dark when they returned to camp. And it was still dark when they left camp early the next morning to bring in their catch.

As they neared the beaver slide where Jim had set his first trap, Jim touched his horse lightly and raced on ahead. He came to the slide and, jumping from his horse, ran down to the water's edge.

"Tom," he called, "here's my first beaver."

The trap was not where Jim had set it, but the float on the water made it easy to spot. It had been carried out into the stream when the trapped beaver had tried to swim back to his lodge. The trap chain fastened to the pole, however, had held the trap securely and the beaver was drowned.

Jim plunged into the icy water.

When Tom rode down to the stream, Jim, dripping wet, held up his catch.

"That's a big one," called Tom. "One of the biggest I ever saw. He must weigh fifty pounds."

"How much will the pelt weigh?" asked Jim.

"Two or three pounds. The pelt will bring about eight dollars in St. Louis. Get your knife ready," Tom added as he dismounted, "and I'll show you how to skin a beaver."

Jim pulled his Green River knife from his belt. "This one is for Old John," he said.

"The castor glands and the tail are for you, Jim."

"That's right," agreed Jim. "Is roasted beaver tail as good as the old-timers say it is?"

"It's better. But none ever tastes as good as your first one. There's something about the thrill of trapping your first beaver that you never forget."

They skinned the beaver, cut off the broad, scaly tail, and removed the castor glands. Jim poured the yellow liquid from the glands into his horn bottle. He would use it to make his own bait.

Jim and Tom went on to their other traps. Tom had a beaver in each of his eight traps. Jim had only three more. His fifth trap had just the hind leg of a beaver and the sixth had not been touched.

"You placed your bait stick too high in your fifth trap, Jim," said Tom. "That's why the beaver was caught by one hind foot. If the bait stick had been placed too low, one of the beaver's front feet would have been caught."

"I'll remember that next time," replied Jim.

When they reached camp they dressed the skins of their beaver. In a big camp regular workers took care of all the skins brought in each day. Major Henry's men, however, were anxious to keep on the move and, in order to save time, each man was responsible for his own catch.

Tom showed Jim how to stretch his pelts on the willow frames. The edges of the beaver skins were carefully sewed to the frames to keep the skins flat. Later when the pelts were dry they were made into fur packs. Each pack contained some sixty skins and weighed about one hundred pounds.

Day after day Major Henry's men pushed on toward Three Forks. They made camp each afternoon allowing themselves enough time to set their traps in the nearby streams.

As the men moved deeper into the land of the Blackfeet they were more and more on guard. Although they often passed bands of roving Indians they were not molested. But that did not mean that they would reach Three Forks without trouble.

The Ride for Help

MAJOR HENRY and his men did not expect to reach Three Forks without a fight. They knew that somewhere along the way they would be attacked by the Blackfeet Indians. They were confident, however, that they would defeat the Indians and then push on to the Forks.

The trappers were partly right. The Blackfeet did attack them. But the outcome of the bitter fight was not at all what the trappers had expected. They were not only badly defeated, but they lost all their fur packs and most of their horses as well. They were forced to return to their fort on the Yellowstone.

The stinging defeat, however, did not discourage the men. They planned to return to the Forks as soon as General Ashley and his new party of trappers joined them.

Although the trapping season was over the men

were busy. The nearby friendly Indians again came to the fort bringing with them many packs of beaver. Major Henry was pleased to trade with them for their fine furs. What he really needed, however, was more horses to replace the ones taken by the Blackfeet. But the Indians did not want to trade their horses, even though they were offered more goods than ever before. Since he could not get horses from the Indians, Henry sent two men to meet General Ashley, who was coming up the river. They were to tell him to buy the badly needed horses on his way.

On a June day, late in the afternoon, Jim was on guard. He stood in the high watch tower of the fort which gave him a good view of the surrounding country. Suddenly his hold on his rifle tightened. Far away he sighted the approach of two mounted men.

"Are they Indians?" he asked himself, "or white men?"

He glanced quickly about. All the trappers had gathered, as they did every night, in the open square of the fort. Some were cooking supper, some were cleaning their rifles, while others were resting. The horses were in the corral and the night guards were already on duty. The heavy gate of the fort was closed and barred for the night.

Jim turned and watched the oncoming riders.

"Hello, there! Hello!" they shouted.

Jim waved his rifle in answer.

"White men coming," he called over his shoulder. Then in a loud voice he called to the riders, "Who are you?"

"Ashley's men."

"Ashley's men," Jim reported.

In an instant Major Henry was on his feet. "Open the gate," he ordered.

The gate was swung open. Two foam-covered horses dashed into the square. The riders dismounted. The older man stumbled forward and would have fallen if a trapper had not caught him. The younger rider, a slim, black-haired man, stood for a minute leaning against his horse.

"I'm Jed Smith," he said gasping for breath. "I have a message for Major Henry."

"I'm Henry. What is the message, Smith?"

"General Ashley—surrounded by Indians. The Rees."

Next to the bloody Blackfeet, the trappers feared the terrible "Rees" as they called the Arikara Indians. At the mention of trouble with the Rees the trappers crowded closer around Henry and the two riders.

"Where is Ashley?" asked the major.

"Down the river," Jed replied between deep breaths. "About three hundred miles from here. Just below the first Ree village on the Missouri."

"Is that where Ashley's party was attacked?" Jed nodded.

"When did the attack take place?" asked Henry.

"On the second of June." answered Jed. "Over a week ago. We tried to get here as quickly as we could, but Indians were all around us. We had to travel most of the time at night. It was a difficult trip."

"Difficult! It was a bad trip," broke in the second rider. He was a Frenchman, well known to the older trappers. "It was a very bad trip, Major

Henry. If I had not trap for you before, I no make trip. But you my friend, so I come."

"I know you are both worn out," said Major Henry. "Come over to the campfire."

The riders followed the major to the campfire and sat down beside him. The trappers, eager to hear every word, formed a silent ring around them.

"Did the two men I sent reach General Ashley before the attack?" asked Henry.

"Yes, they did," replied Jed, "and I think that is one reason why we were attacked."

"I don't understand."

"General Ashley intended to pass the villages without stopping to trade with the Rees. But when your men told him you needed horses he changed his mind. Our party stopped at the first village. After two days of trading we had some fifty horses. We made ready to continue our trip. The general gave orders for an early start the next morning."

Jed shook his head. "But we didn't get started. Before sunrise we were attacked."

Quietly, slowly Jed told of the attack. He had been with the land party of forty men that morning and had been in the thick of the fight. He told how the rifles of hundreds of well-hidden Indians had without warning blazed down upon the men. He praised the brave trappers who had faced the deadly fire and the men who had died. He told how he and the men had finally escaped by swimming out to the keelboats which were anchored in the middle of the river.

"Why didn't your party come on after the attack?"

"The Indians were watching our every move."

"That's not the reason, Smith. You are hiding something from me. What is it?"

"We had only thirty men left."

"Only thirty men!" exclaimed Henry.

"I tell you what happened." The Frenchman did not pay any attention to Jed's signal. "Jed won't say bad things not even about cowards. But I tell you. We leave St. Louis in March. We go up Missouri River. We have everything we need. Two fine keelboats, plenty horses, and more than

hundred men. Mostly greenhorns, yes. But the
general and I think they be smart very soon. They
talk big. Want big Indian fight. Oh, yes, they
want big Indian fight to show how brave they are.

"They get it, too. One big Indian fight," the
Frenchman continued, "and what do they do?
They cry and shake. The general, he try to make
them fight. They cry more and shake all over. But
not my friend here," he nodded toward Jed. "He
so good he could be Frenchman. He fight like me.
Good, you know. I tell you how brave he is."

"Just a minute," said Jed holding up his hand.

"Let him go on," said Henry.

"The general, he so mad at greenhorns." The
Frenchman roared with laughter. "I never see
anyone so mad. He send the cry babies back to St.
Louis. That make only thirty men left. The general, he ask for volunteers to come to you. Not
one old-timer say a word. But one greenhorn say
he go. You guess right. Jed Smith say he go and
he only one who say anything. I get shamed. I
say to myself, 'You let young fellow, who never see
Indian country in West before, be more brave than

you?' Oh, I very shamed. I say I go, too, and so here we are."

As the Frenchman talked Jim leaned over the railing of the tower and listened. He watched Jed Smith. His clothes were torn and covered with dust. The deep lines of weariness made him look far older than his twenty-four years. But Jim did not miss the strength and courage of the young man. He knew that in time Jed Smith would take his place as one of the best of the mountain men.

"Yes, and so here we are," said Jed turning to Henry. "General Ashley needs your help."

"And he'll get it," promised the major. "We will be on our way at sunrise."

Leaving Bastian in charge of just enough men to guard the fort, Henry and eighty men rushed to Ashley's assistance. As they had only a few horses most of the men traveled down the river in canoes.

Jim and Tom rode with the mounted men. Jed Smith was also with them. From the beginning the three men were good friends.

At first Jed had not been popular with the other trappers. They paid little attention to him. He didn't seem to fit into their lives. He was quiet, soft spoken, and deeply religious. He had none of the easy manners of the rough-and-ready mountain men. No man, however, who could ride, shoot, and fight like Jed Smith could be overlooked. Long before the party reached Ashley's camp there wasn't a man who didn't respect him for his courage. And he won their real affection because he was honest, loyal, and a true friend.

After a hard trip of almost two weeks, Henry and his men neared Ashley's camp. They slipped by the Indians late one night and reached camp without being seen.

With his increased force General Ashley attacked. The Indians were finally defeated, but the cost of victory was high. Some of the trappers were killed and many were so badly wounded they had to be taken down the river to the nearest fort.

These were staggering blows to General Ashley and Major Henry. They had already spent thousands of dollars to equip two trapping parties. So far their venture in the fur business was a failure. Bad luck had dogged their footsteps for a year and a half. Should they return to St. Louis and put an end to their unlucky fur company? Or should they try again? If they were to try again, time would be needed to hire more men and to buy horses and supplies.

While the two leaders talked over their plans the men remained in camp. They were troubled and anxious. They sat around the campfires in quiet groups or moved restlessly about.

At one campfire Jim and Tom were seated with a group of men. Bill Sublette, who had returned with General Ashley, was with them. The trappers were glad to see Bill again. Bill's younger brother, Milton, was with them, too. Milton had proved himself a good Indian fighter in his first fight.

The Sublette boys, Bill and Milton, were much alike—tall, good-looking, and popular. They were devoted to each other, and they were both eager to become mountain men. Beneath their happy-go-lucky manners there was the courage needed to meet the tests of the wilderness.

"I don't see why you men should be so upset,"

said Wolf Andrews as he joined them. "What difference does it make if Ashley and Henry call it quits?"

The men made no reply.

"We can always trap for some other company," Wolf continued. "As for me, I'll trap for anyone who pays me the most money."

"You would," flared Tom.

"Well, what's wrong about that?" questioned Wolf. "Aren't you out here to make money, too? Or are you like Jed Smith—out here to explore, make maps, and read the Bible?"

"Leave Jed out of this," said Jim as he rose to his feet.

"Jim, I can take care of myself." Jed's soft voice came from another campfire. "What is it, Wolf?" he asked, coming forward.

Without answering Wolf walked away.

"He will try to make trouble for you," said Tom.

Jed smiled his quiet smile. "No, I think not," he said. "But thanks, boys, just the same."

"Sit here with us," said Tom moving over.

Jed sat down in the circle of men. They were

silent again as they stared into the dancing flames of the campfire.

"You know we are lucky men," said Jed at last. "We have a chance to do a lot more than just trap out here in the West. We can really do something for our country. Have you ever thought of that?"

"No," the men shook their heads.

"Well, we can," replied Jed. "You see, fur trappers are always anxious to find richer beaver streams. In order to find them we must keep pushing on into the wilderness. In our search we can study and explore the country. Think of the good we can do when the settlers come."

"When the settlers come?" interrupted a man. "What in the world are you talking about?"

"People won't come out here to settle," spoke up another. "This will always be our trapping land."

"Once the fur trappers in the East said that about their trapping lands," Jed reminded the men. "But the settlers came. They cleared the land for farms. They built cities and towns. The same thing will happen in the West."

"But it's different out here, Jed."

"Why?"

"Well, the Indians will fight to keep their lands."

"The Indians in the East fought to keep their lands," said Jed. "They lost."

"Well then—" the man hesitated. "Oh, hang it all, Jed, it just can't happen to us."

"We can't stop it," said Jed. "It may be many years before the settlers come. But they will come. They will turn to us and we must help them. By that time the wilderness will be as familiar to us as it is to the Indians. We will know all of it, the rivers, mountains, and valleys. We will have blazed our trails through the wilderness. And over our trails we will lead the settlers to their new lands."

"I don't believe it will ever happen."

"What do you think, Tom?" asked Jed.

"I think you're right," answered Tom. "And when the time comes I'll help the settlers."

"So will I," spoke up Jim.

The men from the other campfires came over and joined the group. Some of them agreed with Jed, but most of them believed that the wilderness would always be their trapping grounds. They were still arguing when General Ashley and Major Henry joined them.

"Are we going on?" the men asked as they crowded around the two leaders.

"Yes," Henry nodded. "We're going on."

Like magic the gloom of the camp disappeared. The men cheered.

"What were you men arguing about when we joined you?" asked the major.

"Well, Jed Smith says that some day the settlers from the East are going to take over our trapping grounds," answered one of the men. "And he thinks we ought to help them do it. He talks about doing something for our country and exploring the wilderness and blazing trails."

General Ashley watched Jed standing before the campfire. He walked over to him and placed a hand on Jed's shoulder. "So we are the trail blazers?" he asked smiling down into Jed's blue eyes.

"Yes, sir, we are," was Jed's quick answer.

Still smiling Ashley turned and said, "Men, I don't believe you quite understand what Jed meant. Maybe I can make it clear to you.

"The early history of the fur trade in America is the story of the English and French fur traders and trappers. The men explored and claimed the land for their countries. England and France fought four wars to gain control of the fur trade. England won, but France will always be remembered as the great pioneer of the American fur trade.

"The settling of our country is closely related to

the fur trade. The first settlers remained along the Atlantic coast. They did not need to go farther west because they had enough land, and game was plentiful near their little settlements.

"As time went on more and more people came to the thirteen colonies. They, too, wanted land, but the best land was already settled. They began to think of the wilderness, the Indian country beyond the mountains.

"Only a few white men knew the wilderness. They were the men, who, like Daniel Boone, had lived there, trapping, hunting, exploring, and trading with the Indians. The settlers turned to them for help. And over the familiar hunting and trapping trails these men led the settlers to the new lands.

"The Revolutionary War stopped the westward movement for a while. But after we won our independence from England more people continued to move into the wilderness. And again it was the fur trappers who led the way.

"There is still enough land for the settlers on the east side of the Mississippi River. But some day

there will not be and then the people will look westward again.   And they will move on and settle the
West.

"We will lose our trapping grounds and the Indians will lose their lands. That will be all right,
I think, because neither the Indians nor we, the
trappers, are builders. The settlers—they are the
builders of our nation.

"But the settlers will need our help. And we
must help them.

"We shall explore the wilderness ahead until it
holds no secrets from us. We shall discover unknown rivers, lakes, mountains, and valleys. We
shall find secret mountain passes.

"That is our place in our country's history. We
are the men who blaze the trails. We are the path-
finders."

———

1.   How did Jim and Tom know when they were near
a beaver dam?

2.   Tell how to set a beaver trap.

3.   How did the beavers make their dams and lodges?

4.   How was the settling of our country related to the
fur trade?

A Secret Mountain Pass

GENERAL ASHLEY returned to St. Louis to hire more men and buy more supplies. Major Henry and the trappers made their way back to their fort on the Yellowstone.

Here they heard more discouraging news. Bastian reported that the Indians living near the fort were becoming more and more hostile.

"I'm sorry to hear this," said Major Henry. "We have had more than our share of bad luck."

"We certainly have," agreed Bastian. "But now that you are back with a strong party of men the Indians may become friendly again."

"Yes, they may. They respect a big party, and the bigger your party the more respect they have."

But as the days passed, the Indians remained sullen and unfriendly. Henry ordered his trappers to stay near the fort. He posted extra men on guard and sent scouts along with the hunting party.

The men were ever on the alert. But a hunting party was attacked by the Indians. More horses were stolen and a night guard was killed.

Major Henry called his men together. "This fall we had planned to return to the Forks. But that is now impossible," he said. "We haven't enough horses to make the trip, and we haven't a chance to buy horses from the Blackfeet."

"We must go back to the Forks," spoke up Wolf Andrews. "We can't let the Blackfeet think we are afraid of them."

"We're not out here to fight Indians. We're trappers," said Henry. "If we should return to the Forks how much trapping do you think we would do? None! We would spend all our time fighting the Blackfeet. I don't intend to waste any more time fighting them. They have chased me out of their country two times and two times is enough."

"That isn't your real reason, Major," said Tom as he stepped forward. "Tell us what it is."

"What makes you think I have another reason?"

"Because I know you, Major," answered Tom smiling. "You wouldn't hesitate for a minute to take another chance at the Blackfeet, if you hadn't already decided on a better plan."

Henry laughed, "You're right, Tom. I have a good reason. Each year other fur companies are sending more men out here to trap. That means two things are bound to happen. With more rivals in the field we will get fewer fur packs, and trouble with the Indians will steadily increase."

"Then where will we go?" asked a trapper.

"I have decided to move on to the mouth of the Big Horn River."

"How will we get there?" questioned Wolf. "If we haven't enough horses to get to the Forks we haven't enough to make the trip to the Big Horn."

"We're headed for the Crow Country," replied the major. "The Crows are always eager to trade with us. They need our guns and gunpowder to fight their Indian enemies. We'll have no trouble getting horses from the Crows. They always have plenty of horses."

"Sure they have," laughed Bastian. "They steal most of them. More than likely they will steal the ones they sell to us."

Check Out Receipt

Dobson Ranch Branch
480-644-3100
mesalibrary.org

Tuesday, March 6, 2018 3:49:16 PM

Item: 185837167
Title: FUR TRAPPERS OF THE OLD WEST
Material: ILL
Due: 03/26/2018

Total items: 1

>>>Visit our Instagram @mesalibrary to vote for
your favorite submissions in our Amateur Photogr
aphy Contest

"Then we'll buy them back again," said the major.

"We should return to the Forks," said Wolf.

"Well, you aren't in command, Wolf. We take our orders from Major Henry," spoke up Etienne Provot. He was one of the few experienced men who had signed up with General Ashley's second party. Quick-tempered, bold, and capable, Provot fought Indians or trapped beaver with the same enthusiasm. "Major Henry is right," he continued. "Our best chance to do some trapping this fall is to go to the Crow country. And I am for getting started at once."

"So am I," said Tom. "The sooner we get there the more time we will have to trap."

"And to explore," added the major. "This fall our exploring trips will be more than our usual search for beaver streams. Somewhere in the Crow country is a pass which leads over the Rocky Mountains. I am determined to find this pass."

"Are we going to trap on the other side of the Rockies?" asked Bastian.

"Yes, as soon as we locate the South Pass."

"The South Pass!" exclaimed Provot. "We'll be wasting our time. Many trappers have tried to find the South Pass and all have failed."

"We must find it," said Henry.

"Why can't we use a pass that is already known to us?"

"Because the South Pass will open up a vast, almost unknown, territory," answered the major. "It is the key to the West. The pass leads directly to the Green River Valley."

Jim, as well as the other greenhorns, had learned to remain silent when the older trappers discussed their plans. But now in spite of himself Jim exclaimed, "The Green River Valley!"

The men turned and looked at him. He grinned and shrugged his shoulders.

"Are you interested in the Green River Valley?" asked Henry.

"Yes, I am," answered Jim. "It's one valley I really want to see."

A trapper laughed. "I have never heard anyone tell you about a new place that you haven't wanted to see."

"I guess that's right," Jim replied. "But I have wanted to see the Green River Valley ever since Old John told me about it."

"I hope we will all see it," said Major Henry. He turned again to the old-timers. "If we locate South Pass it will save us hundreds of miles in taking our fur packs back to St. Louis. By going over South Pass we could then travel across the plains instead of having to follow the Missouri River route."

"Well, now I am in favor of finding the pass," said a man. "It would be a relief to come out here any other way than by poling a keelboat."

The men laughed and agreed that poling a keelboat was not their favorite pastime.

"When we have traded for enough horses, I shall divide the outfit into five trapping parties," said the major. "I have chosen an experienced man to act as captain for each party. The captains will be Fitzpatrick, Provot, Bastian, Andrews, and myself. I guess that's all, men," he added. "We'll get started as soon as we have packed our supplies."

In less than a week the trappers were on their way. Major Henry and his scouts rode on ahead

to keep a sharp lookout for hostile Indians. Guards
rode with the men in charge of the pack animals.
The packs were loaded with trapping and trading
supplies. Most of the men, however, were on foot.

Days later the men reached the Powder River
and made camp. A band of friendly Crow Indians
came to their camp. Many of the braves had extra
horses with them. They traded the horses for
goods.

The warriors who did not have extra horses with
them examined the goods, too. The goods had been
chosen carefully to satisfy the Indians' love for
color and for their needs. There were countless
strings of glass beads, yards of red and blue cot-
ton cloth, and dozens of red woolen blankets. There
were boxes of needles and thread, and ribbons of
every color. Iron and copper kettles were displayed
beside the boxes of small, round hand mirrors. The
braves prized the mirrors. They used them to flash
their signals across the sky when they were on
the warpath or out hunting. But most of all, the
braves prized the guns, gunpowder, and the sharp
hunting knives of the white men.

After the braves had looked over all the goods they held a council with their chief.

The chief, a tall, stately, young Crow came to Major Henry. "My warriors," he said, "like white man's goods." He nodded toward the mounted braves waiting near by and added, "They go get horses. They come back soon. You wait?"

"Yes, I wait," answered the major.

The chief held up his hand. The braves whirled their horses about and galloped from camp.

"Crow good hunters," said the chief. "We go hunt for you."

"Thank you," said Major Henry. "Some of my men can go with you."

"Fine! Fine!" said the chief. "I pick white men." He glanced about. "I take him," he said pointing to Jim. "He look like good hunter."

When the hunting party left camp, Jim was riding in front with the chief. Jim asked many questions about the Crow country.

"No Indian have land like Crow country," said the chief. "Crow country best. Many beaver here. Hunting good. Much grass for horses."

"There is a pass somewhere in your country which leads over the Rocky Mountains," said Jim. "Do you know where it is?"

"No," the chief answered.

"Do your braves know where it is?"

"I not know. They not know."

"But someone must know," insisted Jim.

"My father, big war chief of Crow. He killed by Sioux in big fight. He know about pass."

"What did he say about the pass?"

"All he say it not look like mountain pass."

A yell from the Indians made Jim and the chief rein in their horses.

"Buffalo!" shouted the braves. "Buffalo!"

The hunt was on and the pass was forgotten. Late in the afternoon when they had plenty of buffalo meat the hunters returned to the trappers' camp.

As Jim swung from his saddle, Bill Sublette called to him. "Tom told me to tell you good-by."

"Good-by?" questioned Jim. "What do you mean?"

"He and his trapping party left while you were

out hunting," explained Bill. "Andrews and his men left, too."

"I don't mind missing a chance to say good-by to Wolf," laughed Jim, "but I had hoped that you, Milton, Jed, and I could be in Tom's party."

"Jed went with Tom," said Bill.

While they were talking Provot joined them. "You're in my party, Jim," he said. "We're pulling out in the morning as soon as Major Henry can buy more horses from the Crows."

"I'll be ready," said Jim. "Where are we trapping?"

"Southward along the Powder River," answered Provot. "Then we'll head for the Sweetwater River Valley and trap there, too."

"Good! That's all new country to me."

"I thought you'd like it," grinned Provot, "but let's get one thing straight, Jim. I'm captain of a fur-trapping party and I'm not out to see the country."

"What about trying to find the South Pass?"

"We'll do some exploring," replied Provot, "but I still say I'm captain of a fur-trapping party."

He turned to Bill. "Who was lucky enough to get the Sublette boys?"

"We're with Bastian," answered Bill.

"He's a good captain," said Provot. "Say, he didn't get caught to build the fort on the Big Horn, did he?"

"No," Bill laughed, "and I'm glad of that. I want to do some trapping this fall. Major Henry and his men are going on to build the fort."

"Well, I'll see you there when the weather gets so cold we can't trap any longer," said Provot.

"Have you ever trapped in the Sweetwater Valley?" asked Jim.

"Yes," Provot nodded, "and I'm glad to be heading back there again."

"Then it must be good."

"It is," replied Provot. "I'm expecting my men to bring back the most fur packs. That means you'll have to be 'up to beaver' all the time, Jim. You'll not only have to bring in your daily catch, but you will also have three greenhorns to bring 'up to beaver.'"

"And if I do, may I have the rest of the time to

explore the surrounding country?" asked Jim.

"Well, after you have brought in your traps each day, taken care of your pelts, mended your equipment, cooked, stood guard, and a few other odd jobs you won't have much time to explore."

"No, that won't give me much time," agreed Jim. "But when we are on the march, I could go ahead of the party. Maybe then—"

"That is exactly what you are going to do," broke in Provot. "I'm making you my scout."

"Your scout!" exclaimed Jim.

Provot nodded. "Do you think you can take us up the Powder River Valley?"

"I can do it all right. I know I can."

"I think you can, too," said Provot. "You're no longer a greenhorn. All you need is a chance to prove it and I'm giving it to you." He slapped Jim on the shoulder. "But there is one thing I want you to remember and I don't want you to forget it—not even for a minute. I have twenty-five men in my party. Our lives will depend upon your ability as a scout."

"I'll remember," promised Jim.

The Scout Rides Alone

AT DAWN the camp was astir. While the men were eating breakfast the Crow braves arrived with more horses. The trading goods were unpacked and the trading began. By noon Major Henry had bought enough horses for Provot's party. A short time later Provot and his men were on their way.

Jim was already well in advance of the party. He was pleased and a little proud to have been made scout. But he knew that it was a deadly serious job. There must be no guesswork in his reading of any sign. He must know exactly what he had seen, and when and where he had seen it. One sign overlooked, or the false reading of a sign, could cost the life of every man in the party.

There was little danger of Indian attacks until the trappers neared the Sioux territory farther south in the Powder River Valley. But the Sioux could be anywhere.

Jim was taking no chances. His long, heavy rifle, lying across his saddle horn, was loaded and ready. Watchful, alert, he rode along searching the low hills, the open country, and the high banks along the river for signs of Indians, either hostile or friendly.

Reaching the top of a hill, Jim reined in his horse. Turning in his saddle he looked back at his fellow trappers riding toward him. Captain Provot was in the lead. The mounted men followed in single file. The pack horses, loaded with the supplies, were in the center of the long line.

"There they are," Jim said to himself.

He waved his broad-brimmed felt hat and smiled as Provot returned the salute of the trail. Then, touching his horse lightly, he raced down the hill. All day he kept ahead of the party. Now and then he stopped to study the country more carefully, and to rest his horse.

Shortly before dark he came to a high bluff along the river. "This would be a good place to camp tonight," he said to himself looking all around. "There is plenty of grass for the horses and we can get wood for our fires from the grove of cottonwood trees over there. I haven't seen any Indians, but I will ride on to make sure."

Jim scouted the country on both sides of the river. Finding no Indians or signs of them, he started back to report to Provot. A mile or so downstream he met the captain and his party.

"Well, Jim how do you like being my scout?" asked Provot.

"I like it," smiled Jim. He added, "I have found a place to camp. It's on a bluff and there is plenty of grass and wood."

"That sounds all right," said Provot. "I'll bring in the men. You ride on and scout the surrounding country."

"I've already done it," replied Jim.

"Both sides of the river?"

"Both sides."

"Good for you, Jim," praised Provot.

Riding beside the captain, Jim led the men to the bluff. Camp was made and guards were posted. Jim's scout duties for the day were over.

Day after day the party traveled southward

along the Powder. Jim, in the lead, was ever on the lookout for trouble. As the trappers neared the Sioux territory Jim began to sight Indian hunting parties. He followed their trails to make sure they would not molest his men. He reported to Provot, telling him the number of braves in each band and exactly where he had seen them.

The captain doubled the night guard and the men slept with their rifles beside them. During the day, guards rode on each side of the pack horses.

One morning as Jim was riding along the Powder he sighted the faint marks of a trail in the distance. He followed the trail trying to find some signs which would tell him if the trail had been made by Indians or by another party of white trappers. The only signs he found were the hoofprints of many horses.

The lack of signs troubled Jim. He knew that Indian hunting bands were not careful about hiding their signs. He had often found their deserted camps, the ashes of their campfires, discarded blankets or broken bows and arrows. But

Indians on the warpath, he remembered, were careful not to leave signs.

Tense, alert, Jim rode on. The trail wound its way along the river for several miles. Then it struck out across the open country.

Jim studied the plain before he headed westward over the trail. He rode slowly as he searched for signs. Suddenly he stiffened. Just off the trail and almost hidden in the tall grass was an Indian war shield. From the design painted on the strong buffalo hide he knew the shield belonged to a Sioux brave.

Jim leaned from his saddle and picked up the war shield. He turned his horse about and raced back to the river. He met his party and reported to Provot.

"And this is the shield I found," said Jim when he had told about following the trail. "I didn't see a band of Indians, but they're on the warpath out there somewhere."

"We must locate them," said Provot. "They may try to attack us."

"If you'll let another man scout for the party

today, I'll find the Sioux somewhere," said Jim.

"Do you think you can do it alone?" asked Provot.

Jim nodded. "It may take me all day but I'll locate them," he said. "I'll find our camp tonight."

"All right, Jim. Good luck."

It was late in the afternoon when Jim finally sighted the Indians. They were making camp beside a small creek lined with cottonwoods and willows.

Jim slipped from his saddle and hobbled his horse. Then crawling through the grass he moved nearer the camp. Inch by inch he made his way, moving so slowly that the grass barely stirred. He could now hear the voices of the braves.

Jim listened intently. "Why, it's Tall Bear and his braves." He was about to jump to his feet. But he remembered Major Henry's warning not to trust even the friendly braves. "Tall Bear may not be my friend now that he's on the warpath," Jim said to himself. Slowly and carefully he crawled back to his horse. "But I'm going to talk to him just the same."

Jim unhobbled his horse and swung into the saddle. "Well, old fellow," he said softly, "you may belong to a Sioux brave in a few minutes. But right now, you're mine. Come on, let's go."

Holding his rifle high to show that he was a friendly visitor, Jim galloped toward the Indian camp. The hoofbeats of his horse brought the Indians to their feet.

The braves rushed forward. A shouted command from Tall Bear stopped them. They formed a half circle around him and waited motionless as Jim rode into their camp.

"How!" called Jim.

"How!" repeated Tall Bear. A smile lighted his face as he recognized Jim. "Welcome, welcome," he added. "White trapper welcome to Tall Bear's camp."

Jim dismounted. At a signal from Tall Bear a brave led Jim's horse away.

"You stay tonight," said Tall Bear shaking hands with Jim.

"I cannot stay," replied Jim. "I must get back to my men."

"Where they camp?" questioned Tall Bear.

"Along the Powder."

"Where they trap?"

"We are headed for the Sweetwater Valley."

"You find many beaver there."

"Good," said Jim. He glanced around the camp and turning to Tall Bear asked. "Why are you and your braves on the warpath?"

Tall Bear drew himself up to his full height. "We fight big fight with Crows. We win. We on way home. We wear paint to celebrate big victory. Why you want to know?"

"Because I am the scout for my party," answered Jim. "I tell my captain when I see a war party."

"I not fight your people," said Tall Bear. "You my friend. My braves and I celebrate tonight with big feast. You stay eat?"

"I'll stay for the feast," replied Jim. "Then I must return to my men."

The braves prepared the feast and when it was ready they gathered around the campfire. Jim was given the place of honor beside Tall Bear. At first the braves were quiet, but Jim, with his keen sense of humor, soon had them roaring with laughter.

After they had eaten, Jim said that he must leave. Tall Bear turned to the two braves sitting nearest him. He spoke to them in a low voice. The braves jumped up and hurried away. A few minutes later they returned. The first brave was leading Jim's horse. The second brave was leading a handsome black, spirited horse. The brave had put Jim's saddle and bridle on the black horse.

"This horse for you," said Tall Bear as he and Jim rose to their feet.

"Thank you, Tall Bear," replied Jim stroking the horse's long, silky mane. "What's his name?"

"His name Wasaka. That Sioux for strong. He good fast horse. See long legs, deep chest."

"He's a fine horse," agreed Jim, "I'll take good care of him."

Jim mounted and for a minute felt the horse tremble beneath him. He patted Wasaka and spoke to him gently. When the horse had quieted Jim said good-by to Tall Bear and the braves.

The young, proud Sioux held up his hand. "White trapper and Tall Bear good friends," he said, "We meet again."

"Yes, we will meet again," said Jim.

The Indians shouted their good-bys as Jim rode away, leading his old horse. The night was dark, but Wasaka galloped on, needing only the slightest touch of his new master to guide him.

It took Jim almost two hours to find the trappers' camp. But by heading for the river and then riding upstream he finally reached the camp. Provot and the men were glad to see him. Jim told them about how he had located the Indian camp and about his visit with Tall Bear and his braves. He proudly showed them his new horse, Wasaka.

"Well, boys," said Provot when Jim had finished, "the next time we won't worry about our scout."

Jim laughed, "The next time I might not be so lucky."

———

1.   What was the "Key to the West"?
2.   Why was Henry anxious to discover the "Key to the West"?
3.   What is your idea of a good scout?

Signs along the Trail

BEFORE the sun was up Jim saddled Wasaka and
was on the trail. As usual he left camp while the
men were cooking breakfast. They would follow
in a short time, if he did not return to report
that Indians were near by.

It did not take Jim long to decide that Wasaka
was the ideal horse for a scout. Fast, strong, quick
to obey, Wasaka was also intelligent and reliable.
He didn't race along like the wind for awhile, as
some horses did, and then slow down to a trot.
Nor did he move restlessly about, stamping his feet
and tossing his head, when Jim halted to study the
country. Wasaka stood quietly so that from afar
he and his master would attract less attention.

Jim liked horses. He was always kind to them
and they liked him.

And as Jim rode along he said to himself, "In
many ways horses are like people. If you treat

115

them right they are your friends." He leaned forward in his saddle and patted his horse's neck. "Yes, sir, Wasaka," he said aloud, "you and I are going to be good friends."

With Jim in the lead Provot's party made its way up the winding Powder. The sunny September days were becoming colder and the nights were touched with frost.

The green leaves of the cottonwoods and willows were turning yellow. Flocks of wild ducks and geese darkened the sky as they flew southward. Deer and elk were moving down from their mountain pastures. Buffalo, too, roamed the valley in search of grass and water.

Jim saw the signs of the coming winter months, but he kept looking for others more important to the trappers. He looked for beaver signs along the Powder and up the many little streams flowing into the river.

He was not disappointed. Beaver dams and lodges were plentiful. The signs which pleased him most, however, were those which told him it would be a long, cold winter. That meant the beaver pelts taken during the spring trapping season would be of the finest.

In preparing for the long winter months ahead the beaver had left many signs. Their lodges were plastered over with extra coatings of mud and their dams were made stronger. Tender twigs and logs were piled at the water's edge. Before the streams were frozen over, the beavers would store the twigs and logs near their lodges. The bark was their winter supply of food.

One night, when the men had gathered around their campfire, Provot said, "Well, I guess it's time for us to begin trapping." He turned to his scout, "Jim, we'll make camp early tomorrow afternoon, so be on the lookout for Indians, beaver signs, and a good place to camp."

Jim nodded.

"I'll expect you to do your share of the trapping," Provot continued, "but don't forget your duty as scout comes first."

"I won't forget," Jim replied. "In fact I've been so busy I've almost forgotten about the South Pass."

Provot roared with laughter. "What did I tell you, men?" he asked. "Didn't I say that Jim still thinks we can find the pass."

Jim laughed with the men. He was serious, however, as he said, "Some party is bound to find the pass. It can just as well be our party."

"You're right," spoke up a man. "We have as good a chance as any other party to find it."

"That's true," agreed Provot. "But right now I'm more interested in getting an early start in the morning. Roll in, men, we're breaking camp at dawn."

The men spread their blankets on the ground, and were soon asleep. A million stars beamed down upon the silent camp.

It was still dark when Jim awakened. From force of habit he reached out and touched his rifle lying on the ground beside him. Then rising to his feet he folded his wool blanket into a small roll and tied it with a leather strap. He leaned over, picked up his rifle, and quietly left camp.

He hurried to where the horses were hobbled. As he stood talking to a guard the soft velvety nose of a horse touched his shoulder and pushed him gently.

"Good morning, Wasaka," he said without turning. The horse pushed him again. Jim laughed and placed an arm around the horse's neck. Wasaka whinnied a friendly good morning.

"It's time for us to be on our way," Jim said. "How about it, old fellow, are you ready?"

All morning Jim rode along keeping a sharp lookout for Indians. Early in the afternoon he came to a grove of cottonwoods. He decided it would be a good place to camp. The streams near by were marked with many fresh beaver signs. After scouting the surrounding country he rode back and led his party to the grove.

The pack horses were unloaded and turned out to graze. The heavy leather trap sacks were opened and the traps divided among the men. Provot ordered four men to remain in camp to guard the pack horses and supplies. The rest of the men loaded their traps on their horses and, in groups of three or more, headed for the beaver streams.

Before leaving camp, Jim examined the traps

of his three greenhorns. He gave a bottle of his secret castor bait to each man. When they were ready they mounted their horses and started westward. At the first two streams they met other trappers from their party so they rode on in search of another creek.

After they had ridden several miles, Jim saw a long line of willows ahead. It was the telltale sign that they were nearing another stream.

To the trappers the graceful willows and the wind-twisted cottonwoods were almost sure signs of a river or creek. Often, at the end of a hard day's ride, thirsty, weary men searched for the trees with more care than for Indian signs. Not only would the men find water for themselves and for their animals, but the cottonwoods furnished wood for their fires and, when grass was scarce, the bark of the trees was peeled and chopped to feed their horses.

The little creek, bordered by the willows, was a trapper's paradise. A beaver dam had formed a still pond where the beavers had built their lodges. Near the slides the muddy banks were covered with the fresh tracks of the prized fur-bearing animals.

"We'll trap upstream," Jim said to his greenhorns. "Then if we find any floating sticks or other signs on the water we'll know someone is setting traps farther up the creek. Now, of course, that someone could be a trapper from our own party, or some other party. But you'll keep your hair longer if you remember it is more likely to be an Indian."

The men nodded.

"Always work upstream," Jim continued. "Don't let any of your bait sticks, poles, or floats drift downstream. And another thing—keep your ears and eyes open. Do you understand?"

"Yes," the men replied.

"Good," said Jim glancing up at the sun. "It's a couple of hours before sunset, but I guess we'll get started anyway. I want to show each one of you exactly how to set your traps and that will take time." He motioned to the greenhorn nearest him. "You're first. Get your traps and follow me."

It was almost dark when the third greenhorn

set his last trap. Jim, standing in the icy water, watched carefully.

"How's that, Jim?" asked the greenhorn as he shoved the trap pole into the bottom of the creek.

"You set it all right. But if you catch a beaver you'll lose your trap."

"Why? I set it just like the one I set in that beaver slide over there."

"I know," said Jim. "But no two traps can be set alike. You see, the stream is never exactly the same, so each time you have a different problem." He reached for the pole, gave it a jerk, and pulled it free. "You can't use a pole to anchor your trap here because the creek bottom is too rocky. Why not use that old tree stump on the bank?"

"Thanks, Jim, I'll do it while you go and set your traps."

"I want to see you splash plenty of water around the stump before I go. The beavers, you know, have a keen sense of smell and the faint odor of a human being is all they need to be 'up to trapper.'"

A few minutes later Jim went on alone to set

his traps. The greenhorn waded upstream for some distance, as Jim had told him to do, before joining the other men. Laughing and talking they waited for Jim to return.

"I don't know how many times he made me reset my traps," said one man.

"I have six traps," laughed another, "and I had to reset each one at least twice. But I am glad we are trapping with Jim."

"So am I," spoke up the third man. "He certainly knows all about beaver."

Most trappers who were "up to beaver" were impatient with the young greenhorns. The greenhorns were anxious to learn the art of trapping, but they were often careless and they made many foolish mistakes. The old-timers felt that when they had shown the young men how to set a trap and how to skin a beaver that was all they needed to know.

But Jim was patient and understanding. He stayed with his greenhorns while they set their traps. He never hurried them and he made them feel that they would soon be "up to beaver." He stood by ready to help or ready to praise a job well done. He answered their endless questions and told them many of his secret methods of trapping.

Jim's patience was rewarded. His greenhorns were the first men "up to beaver." Every morning he and his men rode back to camp with more beaver pelts than any other group.

"It's our castor bait," Jim explained.

"It's Jim," said his loyal greenhorns.

Provot's party continued its journey up the Powder. Camp was made each afternoon and the men lost no time in hurrying to the beaver streams. The furs of other animals were not as valuable nor were they as plentiful.

Beaver was the fur most prized by the trappers. Millions of beaver pelts were used to make the fashionable tall beaver hats worn by men in the United States and Europe. The constant demand for the fur kept the price high and steady.

A beaver skin was often used by the trappers in place of money. Instead of saying a knife or gun cost so many dollars, they said it cost so many beaver skins, or plews. Not all beaver skins, however, were called "plews." The skins were sorted and only the finest were classed as plews.

"Plew" was a slang expression used among the trappers. It was taken from a French word which is pronounced the same as plew, but it is spelled "plus" and means "more, the most."

Sometimes Jim's greenhorns thought he was too strict with them. But Jim didn't ask them to do anything he didn't do himself. He was careful in setting his traps and in skinning his daily catch. He insisted that his greenhorns be the same. The work of an expert trapper was rated by the number of plews he brought in.

It was early in October when Provot's party reached the headwaters of the Powder. Jim had led the trappers safely for almost three hundred miles. He was a little anxious, however, as he reported to his captain. The trip up the river was as far as Provot had asked him to scout for the party. Jim hoped to continue as scout. He wondered if Provot had already decided that an old-timer should take over the difficult job.

Jim made his report to Provot.   As always, the captain asked many questions. Jim's answers were those of a scout who knew every detail of the trail. His answers were direct, simple, and truthful.

"Well, Jim," said Provot, "the trip up the river is over. You have done a real job and if you want to be my scout for the rest of the trip, the job is yours. What about it? Do you want it?"

"Do I!" exclaimed Jim. "I certainly do!"

Provot slapped Jim on the shoulder. "There are a lot of good scouts out here in the West. But I'd rather have you for my scout than any old-timer I know. You're keen and alert."

"Well, I try to keep my ears and eyes open."

"It's more than that, Jim. You're a natural-born scout. You have a wonderful memory for signs and places on a trail. I have been up the Powder before, but this is your first trip. I know you could tell me many things about the river I have forgotten or that I just didn't see."

Jim looked back over the trail. His eyes followed the twisting course of the river until it disappeared in the distance. But for him the river flowed

on, winding its way northward. Stamped on
his mind was every turn of the winding, yellow
stream. The valley with its grassy plains, its
rugged badlands, and its great open sagebrush
country was fixed in his memory.

Jim didn't look back for long. He had seen the
Powder River Valley. He was ready to go on to
the new country in the southwest.

"When do we leave for the Sweetwater?"

"Early tomorrow morning," answered the captain.

"Then I must be on the trail at sunrise."

And at sunrise Jim was on his way. "Now for
the Sweetwater," he said to Wasaka, as the handsome black horse raced like the wind over the
trail. "Do you know what that means, Wasaka?"
he asked. "It means we're headed for the Rocky
Mountains—and maybe the South Pass."

---

1. What does "Wasaka" mean in the Sioux language?
2. What fur was most prized by the trappers?
3. What were the finest beaver skins called?
4. What did Provot say about Jim's scouting ability?

Beaver Traps and War Bonnets

THE SWEETWATER RIVER, in what is now the state of Wyoming, is a lovely mountain stream. Some old-timers say the river was given its name because a pack mule lost its load of sugar in the stream. Others say early trappers gave the river its name for another reason. In the surrounding country the waters of the little creeks and streams were too salty to drink. But here the water coming down from the mountains was fresh and clear. Thirsty men drank long and deep and called the water "sweet."

Provot and his trappers were no exception. Their trip across the sagelands had been difficult. They were glad to reach the Sweetwater. They made camp on the north bank of the river at the base of a giant boulder.

The boulder rose almost straight up from the level plain and covered more than twenty-five

acres of ground. At its tallest point it was about
two hundred feet high. The great rock was to
become known as "Independence Rock," one of the
most famous landmarks in the West. Trappers,
and later the Oregon-bound settlers, carved their
names on its sheer walls of granite. Most of the
thousands of names are now gone. But the old
rock, a faithful scout, still marks the trail up the
beautiful Sweetwater.

Jim lost no time in climbing the boulder. At
the top he glanced down at the trappers' camp.
Then he looked out across the valley. Far to the
right a mountain range rose to the blue, cloud-
less sky. The range was not very high nor was
it an important one. But it was the one Jim had
been waiting to see. It was the first, the beginning of the mighty Rocky Mountains.

Jim felt a sudden rush of joy swell within him.
"The Rockies," he cried aloud. "The Rocky Mountains!" Without realizing it he held out his
arms for a minute as though to pull the mountains closer.

While Jim stood looking at the faraway range,

a flash of light in the east attracted his attention. The flash was followed by another. Then, from a point nearer the trappers' camp, three quick flashes shot across the sky.

"Indians," Jim said to himself, "and they are using mirrors to flash their signals. But where are they?"

Not a sign could he see. The Sweetwater was peaceful and quiet. In the distance a herd of buffalo moved slowly over one of the many buffalo paths which crossed and recrossed the fertile valley. The river, bordered by cottonwoods and willows, sparkled in the bright, early morning sunshine.

Jim brought his rifle to his shoulder. At the same instant a flock of birds flew up from the willows on the river's edge. Chattering and scolding the birds circled the willows and in noisy flight winged their way eastward.

"So that's where the Indians are hiding," Jim said, firing a shot into the air. "The sudden flight of birds is always a good sign that they have been disturbed."

He glanced down at the camp. His warning shot had sent the men racing for their rifles. He saw Provot motion to a group of men and they ran to guard the hobbled horses.

"Wasaka," Jim thought. Quickly he turned and, running back to a narrow path, slipped from the top of the boulder down to a lower ridge. Hurrying as fast as he could, he scrambled down the rock. Then tucking his gun under an arm he dashed toward the camp.

"Jim, what is it?" called Provot.

"Indians!"

"Where? How many?"

"East of our camp," replied Jim. "I don't know how many. I saw their mirror flash-signals and the sudden flight of a flock of birds."

"Two very good signs if you know Indians and birds," said Provot. "That was quick thinking on your part, Jim. Now get over there with the men."

"I'd like to see if Wasaka is all right."

"Well, be quick about it."

Jim ran to where the horses were hobbled.

He saw Wasaka and called softly to him. At the sound of Jim's voice Wasaka whinnied. Jim pushed his way through the herd to his horse and removed the hobbles.

"Why are you doing that?" asked a guard.

"If the Indians get us I want Wasaka to have a chance to escape," answered Jim. He put the hobbles in his pocket and stood for a minute talking to his horse.

"Say, Jim," the guard questioned, "you know we may be attacked any minute, don't you?"

Jim nodded, but in the same gentle manner continued to talk to Wasaka. "Now, when the Indians come," he was saying, "don't pay any attention to their war whoops and bright feathers. Remember you're not an Indian horse anymore. You are mine. Do you understand? No more war bonnets for you, old fellow, only beaver traps from now on. That's right. Now, steady Wasaka. I'll be back."

Jim returned to the camp. As he took his place in line with the trappers, Provot said, "I've told the men not to fire until I give the order. I don't want to start a fight but if this is a war party, we're ready."

The minutes dragged by.

"I guess it is a false alarm," said a man.

One of Jim's greenhorns standing next to him lowered his gun. "What do you think, Jim?"

"I don't know, but I'm not guessing about any-thing," answered Jim. "Keep your gun ready to fire."

The greenhorn started to raise his gun. He was too late. A feathered arrow aimed at his heart found its mark. The boy threw up his arms, staggered forward and fell dead.

A war whoop rang out. Over the top of a low hill raced a hundred screaming redskins. Arrows whizzed through the air.

"All right, men," shouted Provot. The figure of a brave was directly in his gun sights. "Let 'em have it."

Twenty-four rifles blazed. Twenty-four Indians pitched forward on their ponies and fell either dead or wounded. Their riderless ponies sped away.

Again twenty-four guns barked. More riderless ponies streaked across the valley. The wild charge of the Indians was broken and they withdrew.

"They'll be back," said Provot reloading his gun. "Are you all right, men?" he asked as he

glanced quickly from one trapper to another.

The men nodded but made no other reply. Tight-lipped and grim they waited for another attack. They kept their guns trained on the yelling braves.

The Indian fight lasted all morning. The braves

charged several times. Each time the deadly fire of the trappers' guns forced them to retreat. Then, at last, they carried their dead and wounded from the field and fled.

Several trappers were wounded, but the young greenhorn was the only man killed. Jim and the two other greenhorns who had trapped with him buried their friend in the shade of a cottonwood.

Provot praised the men guarding the horses. All during the attack the men had kept the animals under control. It was no easy job. The wild war whoops, the shouts of the trappers, and the rifle fire had made the horses half-crazed with fear.

Only Wasaka had stood quietly. When the fight was over Wasaka wandered off to graze. At Jim's whistle, however, the horse came galloping to him.

The trappers remained in camp the rest of the day. But in the early morning they were on their way up the Sweetwater.

Jim as usual was well in advance of the party. He met a band of friendly Crow Indians and stopped to talk to the chief about the South Pass. The chief only grunted in answer to Jim's many questions.

But Jim was not discouraged. That night in camp he said to Provot, "I still think we can find the pass. We can —"

"Forget the pass, Jim," interrupted Provot.

"But suppose we should find it. What would you do then?"

"Do!" exclaimed the captain. "I'd head for the Green River Valley. The streams are so full of beaver you don't need to bother to set your traps. You just wade out into the water and catch them. But we can't hope to locate the pass. We know so little about it."

"We know the pass is somewhere in the Crow country and that it doesn't look like a mountain pass. That helps a little."

"Well, I'm not going to get excited about it," replied Provot. "That is, not until I see the water in a stream flowing westward. When I see that, then I'll know we have discovered the pass."

"It would be proof," said Jim. "All the streams this side of the Rockies flow eastward and the streams on the western side of the Rockies flow west to the Pacific."

"That's right," Provot stretched and yawned. "It's getting late," he added. "Let's roll in."

Trapping as they went, the men traveled up the river valley. It was beautiful with the bright colors of autumn. To Jim it was exciting for, just ahead, the Rocky Mountains blocked the western end of the valley.

He studied the surrounding country. "If I could only find a break in the mountains," he said to himself, "it might lead us to the pass." But nowhere in the range around him could he see a break. Nor did the valley, with its winding little river, give any hint of the pass.

Ahead, as far as he could see, the sand dunes and low sagebrush-covered hills rolled westward. The land rose gently—ever so gently up the foothills of the Rockies.

Jim rode back and reported to Provot. "Captain," he said, "the country ahead of us doesn't look like good trapping grounds. It looks more like a long, wide, treeless valley. But if we go on we may come to some beaver streams."

"We haven't much choice," replied Provot. "I'm for going on."

The men agreed.

Three days later, however, most of the men changed their minds when a blinding snowstorm kept the party in camp all day. They wanted to turn back.

"It's useless to go any farther," one said.

"We haven't enough food," spoke up another.

"We have only melted snow for water," said a third.

"I know all about it," said Provot. "Where do you think I've been the last three days?" He stepped closer to the sagebrush campfire and held out his hands to warm them over the flames. "It's cold." He shivered a little.

"It's getting colder all the time," said the first man. "And all we have is sagebrush, the poorest fuel in the West, for campfires. It burns too quickly and it's too hot and then you freeze."

Provot looked at Jim. "What do you think about turning back?" he asked.

"If I were in your place I would not turn back," answered Jim.

"Why not?" questioned the men.

"If we go back to the Sweetwater, a country we already know, we will never find the pass," answered Jim. "But if we go on we still have a chance to find it. I know the trip is difficult. I'm as cold and as hungry as you are. But let's go on—at least for a few more days."

The men were silent. At last one said, "I suppose you're right, Jim."

"Of course he is," spoke up Provot. "I have said that I would not waste our time looking for the pass, but I was wrong. If we are lucky enough to find the pass, the credit belongs to Jim."

Although it was still snowing in the morning the worst of the storm was over. The men broke camp and were on their way westward.

Long, weary miles stretched on ahead of them. They had but little food and the cold nights added to their hardships. But the men pressed on.

Jim rode alone watching, waiting for some sign of the pass. During the days the sun was warm and it melted the snow. The water flowed in little streams in the snowbanks along the trail. The water was ever flowing eastward, but Jim was not discouraged.

Then, one day Jim pulled Wasaka to a quick stop. He stared at the little stream of melted snow. The water was flowing westward! Unable to believe his eyes Jim slipped from the saddle and knelt beside the gully. How long he knelt there he was never quite sure.

"What's the matter?" Provot's voice brought Jim to his feet. He tried to call an answer but could not speak.

"What is it?" asked Provot as he halted his horse beside Jim and dismounted. "You're white as a sheet. Are you sick?"

"No, Captain," answered Jim. "I just can't believe it, that's all."

"Believe what?"

"Do you remember when we left the Sweet-water I reported to you that the country beyond looked like a long, wide, treeless valley?"

Provot nodded.

"I was wrong. It wasn't a valley, Captain. It was the beginning of the South Pass."

"The South Pass!"

"Yes, and now we're on the very top of it," said Jim. "Look, the water is flowing west."

Provot dropped to a knee beside the little stream. For a long minute he remained motionless. "You're right," he said in a low voice. Then throwing his hat into the air, he shouted, "You did it, Jim! You did it! This is the South Pass!"

---

1.   How did Jim know where the Indians were hiding?
2.   Could the Indians use their mirrors to flash signals at night? When did they use mirrors?
3.   Why did Jim remove Wasaka's hobbles?
4.   What sign did Jim look for when he was trying to find South Pass?
5.   Why did the men want to turn back?
6.   What did Jim tell them?

Jim Bridger — Mountain Man

AT FIRST the trappers did not believe Provot when he told them they were on the summit of South Pass. How could they be, they asked? How could they climb to the mountain top and not know it? They turned to Jim.

"I can't answer your questions," he said to them. "All I know is that we are on the summit and we have discovered the pass. "We—"

"No, not we," broke in Provot. "You, Jim, you discovered South Pass."

It may be difficult for anyone who has not crossed over the pass to understand why the trappers failed to know they were climbing to the mountain top. It may be even harder to understand when we remember that the pass is more than seven thousand feet above sea level.

For those who know the trail, however, it is easy to understand. The rise is so gradual that the

143

steady upward climb is not realized until the flat mountain top is reached.

Jim made no boastful claims when he discovered the long-sought pass. Instead he was modest. He accepted the praises of his fellow trappers lightly.

"I don't deserve all the credit," said Jim. "I just happened to be in the lead."

"Well, I like that," laughed Provot. "You're my scout and I'm mighty particular who scouts for me. You didn't just happen to be in the lead."

"Yes, and the rest of us wanted to turn back," said a trapper.

"Well, all that's important now is that we are headed for the Green River Valley," said Jim. "I hope we won't be disappointed."

The men were not disappointed. Beautiful Green River Valley was a trapper's paradise. The river and the little creeks which flowed into it were rich in beaver. Game was plentiful and there was grass for the horses. The Snake, or Shoshone, Indians living in the valley did not molest them.

For more than a month the men trapped and explored. They wanted to stay longer, but they could not. They still had to make the long trip back to Henry's fort on the Big Horn before the winter snows made it impossible to travel. At first they planned to take their fur packs with them. They decided, however, since they would return to the valley in the spring, to leave their valuable furs in a cache.

A cache, or hiding place, was used to store goods and supplies of all kinds. A cache was usually a deep bottle-like hole in the ground.

To make a cache a thick circle of sod was first cut and carefully removed from the ground. The sod was saved and later used to plug the opening just as a cork or stopper is used for a bottle.

Then the hole was dug and lined with grass, leaves, sticks, the bark of trees, or with wild animal skins. The supplies were packed firmly into the hole and the sod carefully replaced.

The size of the hole depended upon the amount of supplies to be stored. Often a cache was more than six feet deep and from ten to twelve feet wide. The cache was lined to keep the supplies dry and in good condition for many months.

It was not very difficult to make a cache. But to remove all traces of it so the cache would not be found by wild animals, keen-eyed Indians, or by rival fur trappers was a tedious job.

No cover was used to hide the cache. A cover would only attract attention. The trick was to leave the ground looking exactly as it had been before the cache had been dug.

The earth dug from the hole had to be removed. Not even a handful must be left anywhere near the cache. It was a simple matter for the trappers to get rid of the earth because they always worked along a stream. They piled the earth on blankets and skins and threw it into the water where the current carried it away. The grass was brushed and smoothed by hand to erase all footprints. It was slow patient work. The job was not finished until all signs and traces of the cache were removed.

And then even the men who made the cache could not have found it later except for one reason. A cache was always dug near a landmark. It might be a high cliff, a giant old cottonwood tree, a hill, or some other mark easy to find. But whatever it was the trappers depended upon the landmark to guide them back to their cache.

Provot ordered Jim and six men to make the cache for the party. Jim was in charge. It took Jim and his men all one day to make the cache. When it was finished not a sign of the hiding place could be found. It was a perfect job. Only the landmark Jim had selected, a lone cottonwood growing near by, marked the cache.

When the cache was completed the trappers started on their long trip back to the Big Horn. Jim, mounted on Wasaka, was in the lead. The party had no trouble finding the pass nor in climbing its gentle western slopes to cross the Rockies. Then turning their horses northward the men headed for their winter fort.

On the way they trapped and explored. The days were now almost as cold as the frosty nights. Snowstorms and a biting north wind swept across the country. The men continued to trap, however, until ice blocked the streams and kept the beavers in their snug, brush-pile lodges. Unable to trap any longer the men hurried on to the Big Horn.

After days of steady travel, Jim sighted the little fort on the river. He rode back and reported to Provot. The captain called to his men. They cheered and urged their horses to greater speed.

"Bring them in, Jim," said Provot. He touched his horse lightly and raced on ahead.

Almost an hour later Jim and the party reached the fort. Major Henry and Provot were waiting beside the opened gate. Other trappers stood near by, eager to welcome the oncoming riders.

The major signaled for Jim to fall out of line. Jim guided Wasaka to one side and let the men ride on into the fort. He patted his horse and swung from the saddle.

Major Henry strode toward him. "Jim, you've done a real job," said the major.

"Thank you, sir," replied Jim grasping Henry's outstretched hand.

"Provot tells me that you deserve all the credit for discovering South Pass," smiled the major. "He also says you are the best scout he ever had."

"He's a fine captain," replied Jim. He paused

and looked about. "What about the other trapping parties?" he asked. "Have they come in yet?"

"Bastian and Andrews are in with their men, but Tom's party is still out."

"I hope he gets in soon," said Jim. "A few more snowstorms will make it impossible to travel."

"That's true, but we needn't worry. Tom can take care of his party."

While Jim and Major Henry were talking, a dozen or more old-timers edged closer to them. The trappers waited quietly, but the minute the major left they grabbed Jim. They slapped him on the back and shook his hands. They shouted all kinds of greetings; "You old beaver," "You good-for-nothing scout," "You lop-eared prairie dog."

Jim glanced from man to man. In their eyes he saw the true meaning of their rough good humor. They were telling him that they accepted him and that he was one of them. He was—at last—a mountain man.

"Well, what do you have to say for yourself?" Bruce Bastian demanded.

"I—I," Jim tried to answer. He wanted to tell

them that he was proud to be a mountain man and that at all times they could count on him.

"Can't you talk good old United States any more?" a man asked. "Or is the Crow language all you can understand since you discovered South Pass?"

"What about the sign language?" asked another.

Jim held his right thumb and forefinger up to form the letter "O." He touched them to his lips. He made several quick, short, up-and-down movements with his hand held close to his mouth.

"In case you don't know the sign," he said, "it means 'stop talk.'"

The men laughed and crowded around him, that is, all except Wolf Andrews. He had walked away and had joined a group of greenhorns. They paid no attention to him. They were watching Jim.

"Where are the Sublette boys?" asked Jim.

"They are out hunting," answered Bastian. "Why Henry sent those two laughing hyenas out to hunt I'll never know."

"We greenhorns made it," Jim said to himself. "We made it! Now we're all mountain men."

After Jim and the men had talked and joked for some time they went back to their work. Jim put Wasaka in the corral with the other horses. He hurried to help the trappers of his party unload the pack animals.

Jim was glad that his party had reached the fort. But he was worried about Tom. The days passed, some with blinding snowstorms, and still Tom and his men did not arrive. Jim became more and more anxious.

Then, at last one of Tom's trappers, on snowshoes, reached the fort. He brought Major Henry a letter from Tom.

"My men and I are all right," read the letter. "We tried to get to the fort, but our horses could not travel in the heavy snow. Luckily, some Crows asked us to spend the winter with them in their village. We promptly accepted their invitation. We will meet you on the Sweetwater in the spring.

"We had a good trapping season. Our fur packs are well hidden in a cache near this village. We had no serious Indian trouble except two fights which I could not avoid. We won both fights, and after that the Indians left us alone. Once we were almost attacked by Tall Bear and his Sioux braves. When he learned I was a friend of Jim Bridger he called off the attack. We had a feast instead. Tell Jim thanks for me.

"Jed Smith was attacked by a grizzly bear. He was badly wounded before the bear was killed. Jed is slowly improving.

"We have learned nothing about South Pass. I still hope to find it. Maybe the Crows will give me some information this winter."

Major Henry read the letter to the trappers. They were all glad to know that Tom and his party were safe. And Jim, no longer worried, went hunting with the Sublette boys.

The winter months passed quickly. The men had plenty to do. There was always equipment to be mended, buckskin clothes to be made, bullets to be molded, guard duty, hunting, exploring, and endless other jobs about the fort.

Whenever Jim had any free time he saddled Wasaka and rode off to explore the surrounding country. One day when he returned to the fort

Wolf Andrews was waiting and called to him.

"Major Henry wants to see you," said Wolf coming nearer. "He's in his cabin. Here, I'll take your horse."

Jim's hold on Wasaka's bridle tightened. "I'll take care of my own horse," he replied riding on to the corral.

"What's this all about?" he asked himself. He was not thinking about why Major Henry wanted to see him. He was thinking about Wolf. It was the first time during the winter that the Indian fighter had spoken to him. "I don't like it," he added frowning a little. "I feel it means trouble."

Jim hurried to Major Henry's cabin. The major, seated behind a crude table, looked up from the map he was studying. "Sit down, Jim," he smiled pointing to a stool.

Jim sat down, hat in hand.

"I've been talking to my captains," began the major. "I hope to start the spring trapping in a week or two. Each party will trap by itself on the way to the Sweetwater where we will meet Tom. Then, with you in the lead, we'll push on to

South Pass, cross the mountains, and head for the Green River Valley. Now those are my plans, but I want to talk to you about scouting. Provot, of course, wants you to scout for him, but Wolf Andrews wants you this time."

"Wolf Andrews!"

"Yes," Henry nodded, "and I want you to scout for him even though you two are not friendly." He paused. "General Ashley hired Wolf because Wolf was an experienced man and we needed him. But I have never completely trusted Wolf. He has a bad temper and sooner or later he will get into trouble. I want you with him because I can depend upon you. Will you do it for me, Jim?"

"I'll do it for you."

"Good. Now go and report to Wolf."

Jim left the cabin. He closed the door softly behind him. He saw the Indian fighter standing a short distance away watching him.

Jim squared his shoulders. "Wolf," he said striding forward, "Henry told me to report to you."

"Are you scouting for me?" asked Wolf.

Jim nodded. "Yes, I am," he answered.

"Well, you may have scouted to suit Provot, but you'll carry out my orders on this trip. Do you understand?"

"I do."

"And no man in my party ever questions my orders. Do you understand that, too? I won't have—"

"Just a second, Wolf," broke in Jim. "Let's get this straight right now. I'll carry out your orders as long as they are for the good of the party. But I'm warning you not to try to get even with me at the expense of your men."

"What do you mean?" flashed Wolf.

"You know what I mean."

"You still don't trust me, do you?" Wolf laughed.

"Trust you!" exclaimed Jim. "You're right, I don't trust you, but I promised Major Henry to scout for you. I will do my best to protect your party."

———

1. What is a cache?
2. Tell how to make a cache.
3. Why did the trappers need a landmark when they made a cache?

The Sioux War Chief

THE SUBLETTE BOYS were concerned when they heard that Jim was to scout for Wolf Andrews. They went to Jim and urged him to let another trapper scout for the Indian fighter.

"Jim, your life may be in danger," said Milton. "Wolf may try to get even with you."

"I know it," replied Jim.

"Then why scout for him?" asked Bill.

"I have been waiting to prove to Wolf Andrews that I'm not afraid of him," explained Jim. "You see, this is more than a question of scouting. It's a showdown between Wolf and me."

"You're right," agreed Bill. "But I still wish you wouldn't do it."

"And so do I," said Milton.

"What would you do if you were in my place?"

Bill and Milton looked at each other. "You win, Jim," they agreed. "Good luck to you."

A few days later the fur trappers left their winter fort. The parties spread out, each going its separate way.

Jim, leading Wolf Andrews' party, raced Wasaka over the winding trail. The frozen ground was hard and Wasaka's galloping hoofs pounded out good luck! Good luck! Good luck!

"I'll need it," Jim thought. He turned in his saddle and glanced back at the line of mounted men following him. He waved his hat half expecting Wolf to return the salute of the trail. Wolf did not return the salute.

Jim rode on. Good luck! Good luck!

When Jim had scouted for Captain Provot, the job had been made easier by Provot's helpful advice. Jim had quickly won his captain's confidence and respect. Captain and scout had worked together, each believing in the ability of the other.

Jim knew that scouting for Captain Wolf Andrews would be very different. He was determined, however, to do a good job of scouting.

At first Jim had no trouble with Wolf. In

fact, Jim saw very little of his captain. Jim was on the trail early each morning. At night, after he had reported to Wolf, they avoided each other. They seldom spoke except to talk over some scouting or trapping problem.

One night Jim and several men were sitting around their campfire. They were cleaning and oiling their rifles. The rest of the men, rolled in their blankets, were asleep near by.

Wolf joined the trappers at the campfire. He stood watching them. His shadow fell across Jim's gun. Jim moved to get in the light again.

"What's the matter, Bridger?" snapped Wolf.

"Nothing," Jim answered without looking up.

"Come on, Jim," said a trapper rising to his feet. "It's our turn to guard the horses and mules. Are you ready?"

"I'm ready."

The two men left camp. Suddenly Jim stopped. "What was that noise?" he asked, peering into the inky blackness of the night.

"I didn't hear anything," answered the trapper standing beside him.

"Well, I did." Jim brought his rifle to his shoulder.

Something was moving slowly toward the camp. The snapping and crackling in the underbrush came nearer.

"You're right, Jim. Could it be an Indian?"

"An Indian wouldn't make that much noise."

"Then what do you think it is?"

"Some wild animal trying to get to our horses."

Just then in the darkness Jim saw a pair of flashing eyes. He took quick aim and fired. A low moan, a heavy thud then silence told him that his aim was true. He hurried forward.

He stumbled across the dead animal. He ran his hands over the body. For a second Jim held his breath. "I've shot a mule by mistake," he said. "I thought it was a wild animal."

The rifle shot had awakened the camp. Reaching for their guns, the men fled to cover. Now seeing Jim and the trapper walking slowly back to the campfire they rushed out to meet them.

"What was it?" questioned Wolf stepping from behind a tree where he had been hiding.

"I shot a mule by mistake," answered Jim.

"A mule! You blasted bonehead."

"I'm sorry," said Jim. "It was a mistake."

"A mistake! How do you think we'll carry our fur packs if you keep shooting mules by mistake?"

"I know we need our pack animals."

"You'll pay for this," snarled Wolf. "Turn in your horse."

"Wasaka?"

"Why not? You shot a company mule, didn't you? I'll need another animal to carry that pack. Your horse is just the one to do it."

"You can't take a fine horse like Wasaka and break his spirit by making a pack animal of him."

"Who says I can't?" roared Wolf.

"I do!"

Wolf flushed as he met the steady unafraid eyes of his scout. For a minute the two men faced each other, then Wolf looked away.

"My scout must have forgotten that as captain my orders are obeyed without question," Wolf said to the listening men. "But I'll be generous."

He turned again to Jim. "Let's see, you have been out here almost two years now, haven't you?"

"I have."

"All right. You can pay for the mule either by turning in your own horse," sneered Wolf, "or by working the two years for nothing."

"I'll work the two years for nothing," was Jim's instant reply.

The men gasped. What was Jim thinking about? Two years of hard work with no pay just to save his horse? Didn't he remember the long, weary miles on the trail, the beaver streams where he waded waist deep in the icy water to set his traps? One glance at him, however, made them realize that proud, high-spirited Wasaka meant more to him than two years' pay. And with a cheer the men crowded around him.

Wolf, left out of the circle of men, walked away. A few minutes later he saw Jim and the trapper leave camp to take over their guard duty. He heard the men praising Jim and he muttered to himself, "The trip isn't over. I'll get him yet."

The party pushed on, trapping as it moved

deeper into Sioux territory. Jim, ever watchful, rode ahead keeping a sharp lookout for hostile Indians. After spending the long winter in their villages, many bands were on the prowl. The braves were eager for a fight. But because of Jim's careful reports to Wolf the trappers were not molested.

One day when Jim was riding along a stream he sighted a band of Indians farther up the little creek. He reined in Wasaka and slipped from the saddle to the ground. "Stay here, old fellow."

Jim walked upstream keeping close to the willows along the bank. He paused to watch the Indians.

"It's a war party of more than a hundred braves," he said to himself. "But they have been defeated and have made camp to care for their wounded."

The Indians were in full war dress. Even their ponies grazing near by were decorated with the gaudy colors of war. No bloody scalp dance or victory songs, however, broke the stillness of the camp. The warriors in quiet groups waited

before their medicine man. The chief, wearing
the largest feathered war bonnet, sat apart from
his braves. His head was bowed.

"He's praying to the Great Spirit," thought
Jim. "I should say a prayer myself. Indians on
the warpath are bad enough, but a defeated band
is even more dangerous. The chief, in order to
save his pride, will attack the first party he meets.
I must get back to my men and lead them around
some other way."

As he turned a rifle shot split the air. He
dropped to the ground and lay still. In the Indian
camp the braves ran about shouting their wild
war whoops.

"That shot didn't come from their camp," said
Jim to himself. "They are as surprised as I am.
And Indians don't use enough gunpowder to
make that loud a noise. That was a white man's
gun." His eyes narrowed. "And I know only
one person who would try to shoot a man in the
back."

Jim raised his head to see what the Indians
were doing. "Now I'm in for it," he said falling

flat on the ground again. "The chief and some of his braves are coming this way."

When the Indians were only a few yards away they stopped. They talked in low voices for several minutes. Then, following their chief, they turned from the path along the creek and headed for the open plain.

Jim waited until the Indians were out of sight. "I must get to Wasaka," he said as he began to crawl through the underbrush. "I don't want the Indians to find him and run off with him."

But when Jim neared the spot where he had left his horse he saw that the Indians had already found Wasaka. They were laughing and talking to the horse. Jim knew at once that the braves were friends, for Wasaka was standing quietly.

Jim jumped up and ran forward. "Tall Bear!" he called. "Tall Bear!"

Jim had expected one of the braves to answer his call. But it was the chief who turned and held out his hand. "My friend," he said stepping forward, "we find Wasaka. We know you near."

"Why, Tall Bear, you are a chief now!" exclaimed Jim. "I did not recognize you."

"I chief now. My father killed in big fight with Crows. My people make me war chief."

"I am glad. You will be a good chief."

"Thank you, my friend." Chief Tall Bear bowed low. He pointed to Wasaka. "He know me. You care for him good. That show you like him. He good horse like I say?" he asked.

Jim put his arms around Wasaka's neck and hugged him. "He's the best horse in the West."

"You fire gun?" Tall Bear asked.

"No."

"Indian not waste so much gunpowder. White man fire gun. Maybe he try shoot you."

"Well, he missed me, so let's forget about it. I saw your camp and your wounded braves."

Tall Bear's eyes flashed. "We have big fight with Crows. They have more warriors. Soon we fight again. We win next time." He paused. "Where your white trappers?"

"They are following my trail," answered Jim. "We are trapping on our way to the Sweetwater."

"My braves and I trap. We have many furs. I trade them to you for goods."

"My captain will be glad to trade with you. He will—"

"I not know your captain chief," broke in Tall Bear. "I trade with you."

"But it is the captain of our fur party who does the trading," explained Jim. "I will tell my captain that you are my friend."

"I do like you say."

"I will bring my captain to your camp to-night," said Jim.

Jim talked to Tall Bear and his braves a while longer. Then, mounting Wasaka, he rode back to his party. He reported to Wolf, but said nothing about the firing of the gun.

"Is that all you have to report?" asked Wolf.

Jim looked at the Indian fighter for a minute without answering.

"That's all you don't already know about," Jim said at last. "If I were you, Wolf," he added, "I'd do a little target practice. You aren't as good a shot as you used to be."

The War Drums Roll

LATE in the evening Jim and Wolf walked to the nearby Indian camp. Tall Bear, dressed in fine beaded doeskins and a war bonnet of eagle feathers, stood with his braves by the campfire. The flames of the fire lighted up the proud, young chief's handsome face.

"My friend," he smiled at Jim and turning to Wolf added, "I welcome you." He looked quickly back at Jim and then at Wolf again. He was no longer smiling.

"My scout here," Wolf nodded toward Jim, "tells me that you have many fur packs and that you will trade with me."

"No, I keep furs." Tall Bear folded his strong arms across his chest.

Wolf turned to Jim and said in a low voice, "I want those furs. See what you can do about it. Tell him I promise that you can trade with

168

him. Promise anything, but get those furs."

"Tall Bear," said Jim, "my captain says that I can trade with you."

"Good! Good!" Tall Bear stepped closer to Jim. "I trade with you."

Since the Indians were on the warpath, they did not have their fur packs with them. Tall Bear said that he would send some braves to get the packs which were hidden in a cache near their winter village. The village was many miles away and Tall Bear explained that it would be several days before the braves could return.

"We will wait," said Jim.

"Fine." Tall Bear bowed. "My friend, you go hunt with me in the morning?" he asked.

"I'd like to go," Jim answered. "I'll be ready after I bring in my traps and—"

"I'll go with you," interrupted Wolf.

"No," Tall Bear's voice was sharp. "We go alone."

"I'll meet you here in the morning," spoke up Jim quickly. He felt Tall Bear's hostile manner toward Wolf and he was anxious to avoid a quarrel between them. "Good night, Tall Bear." Turning to Wolf he added, "We'll go back to our camp."

As they walked through the darkness Wolf sneered, "That redskin! He thinks because he's a chief he can insult me and get away with it. I'll show him that he can't. I'll show him."

"How?" questioned Jim. "By trying to shoot him in the back?"

Wolf, furious with anger, shouted, "That's none of your business!"

"But it is my business," replied Jim. "If you mistreat Tall Bear in any way, you'll settle with me. Do you understand?"

"How dare you tell me what to do?"

"Tall Bear is my friend. Now get this, Wolf, and get it straight. I'll not stand by and watch you try to cheat him."

Wolf laughed, but it was a scornful laugh. He strode on, leaving Jim behind.

When Jim reached camp he joined the trappers at one of the campfires. "What's the matter with Wolf?" a man asked as Jim sat down beside him.

Jim shrugged his shoulders. He made no reply.

"He's losing his grip on himself," said the man. "And that is bad for an Indian fighter."

"It certainly is," agreed another man. "Wolf has changed a lot on this trip and it worries me. I've seen other captains lose their temper. They become reckless and get their men into trouble. That's what is happening to Wolf."

Jim hesitated. He had not discussed his own troubles with the men for he felt that he could take care of himself. But now he knew that by remaining silent the lives of his fellow trappers might be in danger. He drew a deep breath.

"Wolf is trying to get even with me," he began. He told them about his quarrels with the Indian fighter and about their visit to Tall Bear's camp. "It has taken Wolf a long time to realize that he can't bluff me. But he knows it now and he is desperate. Any man who is desperate is also likely to be reckless. He will risk his own life and often the lives of others to get his own way."

"But why should he be angry at Tall Bear?" a trapper asked.

"For no reason except that Tall Bear is my friend," answered Jim. "If Wolf should mistreat him, we're headed for trouble."

"Oh, I don't think it's that serious," said a trapper. "You're just too anxious, Jim."

"I hope you're right."

In the morning Jim brought in his traps and stretched the beaver pelts. Then, mounting Wasaka, he rode to Tall Bear's camp. The chief was waiting for him. A few minutes later they were on the trail.

During the next few days Jim spent as much time as he could with the young Indian chief. They hunted and trapped together.

When the warriors returned with the fur packs Tall Bear invited the trappers to a feast. He was polite to Wolf, but it was Jim who sat in the place of honor beside the chief.

The feast and story-telling ended and the trading began. The fur packs were opened. Jim examined the furs while the Indians looked over the trading goods. The boxes of sturdy, sharp knives, small hand mirrors, yards of brightly colored cloth and many other articles filled them with delight.

Jim was fair in what he gave the braves for their furs. The Indians were pleased. They had not expected the bright glass beads which Jim had given them as small gifts to take to their squaws. But Jim understood the Indians and he knew they valued his friendly act more than the gifts.

When the trading was over Tall Bear came to Jim. "My braves and I thank you. My beads I take to my son. He papoose now. Some day he be chief."

Jim smiled. "I hope your son will like them. Now we must say good-by, Tall Bear. But we will meet again."

"We meet again."

As Jim and Wolf walked back to the trappers' camp Wolf said, "You could have had all their furs for half the goods you gave them. Why didn't you do it?"

"I've never cheated a white man," replied Jim, "and I don't intend to cheat an Indian."

"Well, I intend to get back half of the goods."

"You can't do it, Wolf," protested Jim. "Tall

Bear and his braves traded with me in good faith because of your promise."

"Hang my promise!" shouted Wolf. "What do I care now that I have their furs. And as your captain I order you to tell that Indian chief to return half the goods."

"I refuse to obey your order." Jim's voice was low, but firm. "I told you once I would never carry out an order that would put the lives of my fellow trappers in danger. And that is exactly what you are trying to do. You know, as well as I do, that the Indians will fight, if they think we tricked them."

"I guess you're right," said Wolf. "Well, we're breaking camp. Get on the trail."

A few minutes later Jim was on his way. He rode past the Indian camp and waved to the braves. Then, touching Wasaka lightly, he headed for the low hill leading to the trail.

Jim had gone only a mile or two when he heard the hoofbeats of a galloping horse behind him. He turned in his saddle and recognized the rider as one of the trappers.

"Jim!" the trapper called. "Get back to camp!"

Jim whirled his horse around. He raced back to the trapper. "What's happened?" he asked.

"It's Wolf," the man explained. "He's gone to Tall Bear's camp to demand that the Indians return half the goods. That means trouble, Jim. The men sent me on to bring you back to camp."

Jim held up his hand. "Listen," he said. From across the plains came the roll of war drums.

"You're the only man who can help us now, Jim."

"Come on, Wasaka!" Jim cried. "Come on!"

Like the wind Wasaka sped back over the trail. The war drums rolled again and Indian war whoops rang out.

Jim reached the top of the low hill overlooking the camp. He reined in Wasaka and pulled himself up in his stirrups. Near the edge of the Indians' camp he saw Tall Bear and Wolf. Tall Bear, mounted on his horse, signaled to his braves. They formed their ponies in a long line behind him and remained motionless as statues. A short distance away the trappers were standing behind a mound of boxes and fur packs.

"Tall Bear!" Jim called. "Let me talk to you."

The chief raised his hand. "My friend," he called in answer. He signaled to his braves and started to ride toward Jim. The war drums rolled softly and died away.

"It's Jim!" the cry went up among the trappers.

"I'm back just in time," Jim thought as he rode down the hill. He looked to see where Wolf was waiting. He did not see him.

A rifle shot shattered the sudden stillness. Tall Bear pitched forward in his saddle and fell to the ground, dead. The eagle feathers of his war bonnet were stained with blood.

From behind a tree a black puff of smoke betrayed the spot where the killer had stood. The braves screaming and yelling spread out to make a circle around the tree. Kicking the sides of their ponies the Indians closed in shouting their war whoops. The rays of the sun flashed from their tomahawks and long knives.

"Jim! Save me!" came Wolf's cry for help.

But it was all over for Wolf Andrews, the Indian fighter. The circle of warriors had closed in on

him. When the braves spread out again, Wolf's lifeless body lay drenched in his blood.

Then like lightning the braves raced toward the trappers. The bark of the white men's guns split the air.

"How can I get to my men?" Jim asked himself. "There is only one thing to do, ride for it."

Leaning forward in his saddle he whispered, "Get going, Wasaka."

The horse obeyed. Indian arrows whizzed passed as Jim broke through the circle. The blazing guns of his own men blocked the way. But Jim did not hesitate. Straight toward his men he rode and, with Wasaka at full speed, he jumped from his saddle and fell behind the mound.

"Hold your fire, boys!" he cried. He stood up and called to the braves, "I am your friend. Do not fight my people."

The Indians stopped circling. They rode in toward Jim.

"You trick us," shouted a brave.

"No! No!" Jim dropped his rifle and stepped forward. "Let me talk to you."

"Why you trick us?" asked another brave.

"I did not trick you," answered Jim. "Believe me I am your friend. Do not blame me nor my men for the treachery of our captain. We do not want to fight you. You are all fine braves worthy to be the warriors of the great chief Tall Bear. He would not want you to fight my people."

"True! True!" shouted the braves.

"Then let us be friends."

The braves looked at one another. They held a council and at last one brave rode forward. "We do like you say."

The brave motioned to the other warriors. They rode back to their dead chief and dismounted. Sadly they carried the body of their beloved young chief to their camp.

Quietly Jim and the trappers watched them. When the braves began to sing their death song Jim bowed his head.

At last he said, "Bury Wolf," and in a low voice continued, "I'm going to Tall Bear's braves. They mourn the death of their chief, and so do I. Tall Bear was my friend."

Loyalty of Mountain Men

THE TRAPPERS, after making Jim their captain, moved on through the wilderness. Roving bands of hostile Sioux kept them ever on the alert. But Indians or no Indians the men continued to trap. Often they remained in one camp several days to trap the nearby streams. When they reached the Sweetwater the other parties were waiting.

Jim had barely time to swing from his horse before the Sublette boys were slapping him on the back. "Jim!" they shouted in their noisy, friendly manner. "You made it! You made it!"

"Sure I made it," Jim laughed.

"Where is Wolf?" asked Bill.

Jim didn't have a chance to answer for at the same time the shout of, "Jim's in! Jim's in!" rang out in camp. At once a dozen men started running to meet him. Tom, Bruce, and Jed were in the lead.

When the greetings were over Major Henry said, "Jim, you led the party into camp. What happened to Wolf?"

"He was killed in a fight with Tall Bear's braves."

"Tall Bear? I thought he was your friend."

For a minute Jim made no reply. But his eyes had narrowed and his lips were pressed together in a hard, thin line. "Chief Tall Bear was a friend of any white man who treated him fairly," he said at last. "Wolf killed him—shot him in the back."

"In the back!" the men exclaimed.

Jim told them briefly how he had found Tall Bear's camp and how he had traded with the Indians for their fur packs. He told them of Wolf's broken promise. As he finished he said, "Tall Bear was a good chief. His braves loved and respected him. They attacked us to avenge his death and I don't blame them. Tall Bear," his voice broke, "was my friend."

"He certainly was your friend." Tom put a hand on Jim's shoulder. He waited awhile then asked, "What kind of trip did you have, Jim?"

"A good one."

"Jim, I'd like to inspect your packs," spoke up Major Henry. "I plan to get started in the morning on the trip back to St. Louis."

After the major had inspected the furs he said, "Your packs are in excellent condition, Jim."

Jim felt the major's keen eyes searching him.

"I've been talking to your men," Henry continued. "They think a lot of you, Jim, and so do I. They told me how Wolf Andrews treated you when you shot a company mule by mistake. They also said he demanded that you pay for the mule by turning in your own horse or by working two years for nothing. They tell me in order to save Wasaka you decided to work without pay. I can't let you do that, Jim."

"I'll do anything, Major, but I can't give up Wasaka. He's mine—he's all I have."

Henry smiled. "Of course, he's yours, Jim. But I can't let you work two years without pay."

"Well, I can't take the money," Jim replied.

"Why not?" questioned Major Henry.

"Wolf and I made a deal. He let me keep Wasaka. I must keep my part of the bargain."

"All right, Jim, come with me. I want to talk over some plans with my captains."

Jim hesitated. "But I'm not a captain."

"Your men made you their captain."

"That was only for the rest of our trip."

"You're Captain Jim Bridger from now on."

Jim smiled quickly. He was serious, however, as he asked, "You're not doing this because I—"

"I'm making you a captain because you earned it," broke in Henry. "You have proved yourself worthy of leading your own party. The same is true of Jed Smith, and he is a captain now, too."

Major Henry and his captains discussed the problem of getting the furs back to St. Louis. It was decided that the major and a strong party of men would leave in the morning with the fur packs. The men would guard the pack animals on the trip across the plains to the Missouri River. Here the fur packs would be put on board a keelboat and floated downstream to St. Louis. Only a few men would be needed on the river trip. The rest of the trappers would then be free to do as they wished during the summer months.

"But you captains will have plenty of work to do," said Henry. "I'll expect you and your men to explore the Green River Valley."

"That suits me," grinned Tom. "I'm anxious to return to the Green."

"Return to the Green?" questioned Jim.

"Yes, my party trapped there this spring."

"Then you discovered South Pass, too!"

"Tom found the pass without knowing you had already discovered it," said the major.

"Why, that's wonderful, Tom," shouted Jim. "We both found it!"

"I didn't know you had discovered the pass until we were on our way back to the Sweet-water," said Tom. "We met Provot and his men. He told me."

"We were bringing in the furs we had cached in the valley, Jim," said Provot. He laughed as he added, "Say, Jim, that cache you made was certainly a good one. It took us all one morning to find it."

"You remembered the cottonwood tree was the landmark, didn't you?" asked Jim.

"Sure, but even then the cache was hard to find."

"Were the fur packs and gunpowder in good condition?"

"The packs were perfect," answered Provot. "The gunpowder was a little damp, but we spread it out on blankets and dried it."

"Jim, I wish you'd look at the map I made of South Pass," said Jed pulling a worn Bible from his pocket. He opened the Bible to the map he had drawn on a blank page. "See, this is the pass and here is where we trapped."

Jim studied the map carefully. "It's a good one, Jed," he said at last. "I remember all of it." He handed the Bible back to Jed. "You know, for the first time in my life I'm homesick. I'm homesick for the Green River Valley."

"We will all have a chance to see it," spoke up Bastian. "And for a year or two the valley will be ours. But other fur companies will find the pass and send their men into the valley to trap."

"That's true," agreed Jed, "and that's why I want to go on and explore the Northwest. When other fur companies come to the Green we'll move on to another territory."

"The English firm, Hudson's Bay Company, have a strong hold on the Northwest," said Major Henry. "The English trappers may make trouble for you, if you go to the Oregon country."

"Yes, I know," replied Jed, "but Oregon doesn't belong to England." He shrugged his shoulders. "And I don't think it ever will. The English trappers don't settle in their fur-trapping lands. They want to keep them a wilderness. But we Americans are different. We push on to new frontiers. Some day our settlers will take over the Oregon country and claim it for the United States."

"It would be a great thing to have Oregon a part of our country," said Bastian. "But, Jed, I wish you'd stop talking about your settlers. They are going to put us out of business."

The men laughed. When they were quiet again, Henry said, "Don't worry, Bastian, it will be years before the settlers put us out of business.

In the meantime we have plenty of work to do. Now I want you four captains," he nodded toward Jim, Tom, Provot, and Bastian, "to explore the Green this summer. You and your men are to locate the richest beaver streams so we won't waste any time searching for them this fall."

He turned to Jed. "You and six men are to go to the Oregon country. Don't get into any trouble with the English, but take a look around."

"I'll do that," replied Jed.

"Well, I guess that's all." Henry smiled at his captains. "Good luck to you—to all of you."

In the morning camp was broken. Major Henry and his large party of men guarding the fur packs headed eastward across the plains. The rest of the trappers rode westward for South Pass and the Green River Valley.

On the trip westward the captains and their men had a good time. They were all friends and they were like boys together on a vacation. The long miles of each day's ride were broken by buffalo hunts and at night in camp they laughed and sang around the campfires. Even Jed, more

serious than the others, enjoyed the freedom of
the summer months.

But the men were not careless. They knew too
well the dangers of the wilderness. They were on
the alert. When on the trail, scouts rode ahead
keeping watch for Indians, hostile or friendly.
At night guards stood at their posts protecting
the horses and sleeping men.

One day the scouts, the Sublette boys, reported
that they had met a band of Crow Indians. The
Crows told them they had been attacked by a band
of Sioux braves. Some of the Crows had lost their
horses in the fight.

"The Crows will now try to steal some of our
horses," said Bill. "They will—"

"We'll need extra guards on duty tonight," interrupted Milton.

"Extra guards won't stop the Crows." Jed
laughed a little. "The old horse thieves!"

"More than likely the Crows have already
spotted our camp," said Jim, "so we won't stay
here. We'll cook supper, leave our campfires
burning and ride on for another five or six miles."

The men agreed. They cooked their suppers and waited until it was dark. Then, after throwing more cottonwood logs on the campfires, they mounted their horses and rode away into the darkness.

The trick worked. The Crows did not find the new camp. The following day, however, the trappers rode straight into an ambush of the warring Sioux. Taken completely by surprise the men fell back under the shower of feathered arrows.

"If we run they'll follow us," said Provot. "But if we close in on them, they'll scatter. Come on, men," he ordered. "Follow me!"

The men obeyed. Firing their guns, they rode toward the Indians. Another shower of arrows sent them reeling back. In the charge several men, including Provot, were wounded.

"Bastian, take over," called Provot. His face was white and drawn with pain.

Bastian nodded. He turned to the men. "We'll divide into four parties." He spoke quietly, but Jim noticed that his eyes, usually smiling, were now deadly serious. "Tom, you and your men

close in on the right. Jed, you and your men close in on the left. Jim, your men and mine will take it head-on. Spread out and when I give the order to fire let the redskins have it."

The men raced their horses into position. Bastian waited to give the order.

A war whoop split the air. The Sioux kicking the sides of their ponies streaked across the plains.

"Fire!" shouted Bastian.

Rifles blazed. The men leaned forward in their saddles reloading their guns as they closed in on the Indians.

Jim touched Wasaka lightly and the horse broke into a gallop. Jim raised his rifle. He was about to fire when an arrow struck him in the right arm. The gun dropped from his hands and his arm hung helpless. Blood stained his buckskin shirt. He fell forward and for a minute clung to Wasaka's neck. Then he fell to the ground.

Bruce, fighting with his men, saw Jim fall. He whirled his horse about and raced to help his friend. Even before he reached the spot where Jim lay he swung from his saddle.

"I'm all right," Jim said gritting his teeth.

"Sure you are, but you're out of this fight," Bastian replied cutting the arrow shaft with his sharp knife. "Come on." He helped Jim mount Wasaka. "Now get back to Provot. Have someone remove the arrowhead and bandage your arm.

Get going, Jim. I'll see you a little later."

As Jim rode to safety Bruce turned back to the fight. Two Indians closed in on him. He lifted his gun and fired. One Indian staggered forward and fell dead. Like a flash the other Indian, with upraised tomahawk, was upon him.

That night after the trappers had finally defeated the Sioux they buried young Bruce Bastian. They buried him where he died, trying to help his friend, Jim Bridger.

The men formed a circle around Bastian's grave. They stood with bowed heads while Jed repeated the Lord's Prayer. Then silently they went back to their camp, leaving Jim alone in the darkness.

Jim, his right arm wrapped in a bandage, knelt beside the new grave. "Good-by, my friend," he said in a low voice. "Good-by, Bruce Bastian, mountain man."

----

1. Tell how the fur packs were taken back to St. Louis.
2. Why was Jed Smith anxious to explore the Northwest?
3. How did the mountain men prove their loyalty to one another?

The First Rendezvous

IN THE MORNING Jim, Provot, and the other wounded men insisted that they were able to continue the trip. Camp was broken and the trappers were on their way. As they rode past Bastian's grave each man removed his hat in tribute to the gallant captain. Then touching their horses lightly they galloped away to the West.

Days later they reached the Green River Valley. The captains formed their parties and set out to explore. The trappers of Bastian's party elected Davy Jackson, the most experienced man in their group, their new captain.

To Jim, now fully recovered, the summer was a perfect one. From the beginning he had loved the Green River Valley and now to be back was a delight. He and his men explored the river and the rushing mountain streams pouring into it.

Everywhere along the waterways they found

the telltale signs of the beaver; the gnawed trees, the dams, and the still, quiet ponds where the beavers had built their lodges. They saw the slides, the countless pigeon-toed tracks of old beavers and their kittens on the muddy banks, and other signs familiar to keen-eyed trappers.

The summer months passed quickly and once again the fall trapping season began. The men knew they would have a good season, for all the parties had reported that the Green was a trapper's paradise.

"The Indians here are friendly," said one old-timer. "That is, they are friendly now."

Although the Indians did not molest them the men were taking no chances. Time and again Jim warned his party. "Where you see no Indians, that's where they are. When you think they won't attack, that's when they do attack."

The trapping was even better than the men had expected. The parties remained in the field until ice blocked the beaver streams. Then, after hiding their fur packs in caches, the men made for their winter camp.

The winter, as always, made the men restless. Life in camp was dull in comparison with the exciting adventures they shared on the trail. They were busy, however, for besides the endless duties about the camp they hunted, explored, and did some trading with the Snake Indians living in the upper part of the valley.

The winter was almost over when Jed Smith and his men joined the trappers. Jed's exploring trip to the Northwest had been worth-while. The country was rich in beaver, and he had made maps of the rivers and streams.

A few weeks later General Ashley arrived from St. Louis. He brought with him a large train of pack mules loaded with many cases of supplies. The train was guarded by a strong party of men. After the general had a long talk with Jed Smith, he called the trappers together.

"Men," he said, "I am sorry to tell you that Major Henry has retired from the fur business. He is a fine man and we shall miss him. Our repeated losses discouraged him. He sends his best wishes to all of you, however, and to my new partner in the Rocky Mountain Fur Company."

He paused. "My new partner is a man you all know and admire. I am lucky to have him as my partner. I shall let him tell you of our plans." He turned to Jed Smith. "All right, Jed," he nodded, "take over."

Jed stepped forward. "Fellow trappers," he began. The rest of his words were drowned out by the cheers of the men.

Smiling, Jed held up his hand. When the men were quiet he said, "General Ashley and I have decided to try a new method of buying fur packs. Each spring the Indians and free trappers have many fur packs. To sell them they have to travel to distant trading posts. As our company now has no trading posts, rival fur companies buy most of these packs."

"Are you planning to build a trading post here in the Green?" asked Jim.

"No, we have a better plan," answered Jed. "We will take our trading goods to places where the trapping is best. When the spring season is over we will hold a meeting."

"Oh, I understand," interrupted Provot. "It will be a—a," he hesitated trying to find the right word. "A rendezvous!" he exclaimed. "That is what we French say when we agree to meet at a certain place at a certain time."

"That's it," Jed nodded. "We will let the Indians and free trappers know when and where we will hold our rendezvous. They will come and trade with us."

"It will save time and money," spoke up Bill Sublette. "It sounds like a good business plan."

"The fur trade is an important business," replied Jed. "The general will remain in charge of selling our fur packs and in bringing supplies to us. I shall carry on Major Henry's work here in the mountains. The captains of our trapping parties will be directly responsible to me." He paused and, smiling at Bill and Milton Sublette, added, "You Sublette boys will both be captains and have your own parties this spring. Some of the men who came out with General Ashley will trap with you.

"I guess that's all, men," he added. "There is one matter, however, I want you to remember.

We will spend more time exploring." He glanced toward Jim. "I thought that would please you, Jim," he laughed.

Jim grinned. He said to Tom standing next to him, "He's all right!"

"He certainly is," agreed Tom.

Spring came at last to the beautiful Green River Valley. The men brought in their fur packs from the caches. After the pelts had been aired and brushed, General Ashley examined them.

One day as he was looking over the furs he asked, "Who brought in these packs, Jed?"

"Jim Bridger's party," answered Jed checking through the company's record book. "Why?"

Ashley sat down on a pile of beaver skins. "You know," he said looking up at his young partner, "Jim's packs will bring top prices in St. Louis. We'll make more money if we sort our furs here and take only the good packs with us."

"You're right, General," said Jed. "A mule can carry only two packs and they can just as well be two good ones."

"Go get Jim. I want to talk to him."

"Here he comes now." Jed pointed to Jim striding toward them.

"You're the man I want to see," the general greeted Jim. "Your fur packs are the best we have. You must have graded them carefully."

"I did," replied Jim. "I put our plews in separate packs. The pelts which were good but not perfect I put in other packs. The rest," he hesitated, "I just threw away."

"Why did you do that?" questioned the general.

"Well, I don't see any sense in taking anything but good furs to St. Louis," explained Jim. "It's a long, hard, expensive trip. Maybe I was wrong to throw away the damaged pelts but I — "

"You did exactly the right thing," interrupted Ashley. "We are going through all the packs again and throw out the damaged pelts."

The furs were graded and made into packs. Each pack contained some sixty beaver skins and weighed about one hundred pounds. At the rate of six to eight dollars a pelt, each pack was worth from four to five hundred dollars.

When the packs were ready General Ashley and

most of the men he had brought with him left for St. Louis.

Even before the general's mule-pack train disappeared from view the trappers were heading for the beaver streams. The parties moved out in different directions.

The discovery of South Pass, the "Key to the West," had given the Rocky Mountain Fur Company trappers an advantage over the trappers of other fur companies. But Ashley's men knew their rivals would soon follow them into the Green River Valley. Both General Ashley and Jed had urged their captains to explore the lands beyond the Green.

For business reasons it was wise to be ready to move on to untrapped regions. That was why Ashley's men, trapping as they went, pushed on. The discoveries they made and their long exploring trips paid them well. Rich beaver lands lured them ever on to new regions. Through the trackless wilderness they blazed their trails— north, south, and west.

Under General Ashley and Jed Smith's able

leadership the Rocky Mountain Fur Company became famous throughout the West. Its captains, scouts, and trappers were the best of the mountain men. And even its fur packs were the finest.

The furs were so fine that the buyers from the East and from Europe outbid one another whenever Ashley's fur packs were on sale in St. Louis. It was not long before the buyers began to call all beaver pelts of extra beauty "Ashley Beaver." The term was used for years in the fur trade of America.

In July of 1825 the company held its first rendezvous. The news of the rendezvous in the valley of the Green had spread far and wide. The free trappers, singly or in pairs, came riding in with their fur packs.

Bands of Indians set up their tepees and made camp. The Indian squaws and their black-eyed children stared with wonder at the countless boxes of the white man's trading goods.

The rendezvous, or "The Fair of the Mountains," meant more to the trappers than a chance to trade for fur packs. It was a chance to see

old friends, Indian and white again, to sing and laugh and celebrate all day and all night. The men played games, raced their favorite horses, went hunting, and spent their year's wages without a thought.

But with all the celebrating there was much work to be done. Jim and Tom were in charge of grading and sorting the furs. The Sublette boys worked with Ashley and Jed during the trading hours. Other men hunted, keeping the trappers

supplied with game. Guards were ever on duty.

Late one afternoon Jim and Tom joined the men in a shooting match. The watching Indians marveled at the expert shooting of the white men. One by one the men lost out until only Jim and Tom were left in the contest.

The target, an Indian war shield, was moved farther away. Jim took his place, loaded his gun and, after taking careful aim, fired. The aim was true. The Indians and trappers cheered.

"Try to beat that shot, Tom," called a trapper.

"I hope I can," grinned Tom. "I'm almost out of gunpowder, and at two dollars a pound it's too expensive to be shooting with Jim."

Another shield was put in place. Tom raised his gun to his shoulder and sighted the center of the target. He squeezed the trigger.

With a deafening roar Tom's gun exploded. The powerful kick of the gun sent him staggering backward. He fell to the ground.

"Tom!" cried Jim rushing to him. "What happened?"

Tom tried to sit up, but fell back groaning. "It's my hand, my left hand."

Tom's left hand was shattered. The exploding gun had ripped the flesh to the bone and one finger was missing.

The torn, bleeding hand made Jim wince. But his voice was quiet as he said, "I'll take care of you, Tom. You'll be all right." He glanced up at the circle of white men and Indians around him. "Come on," he said, "help me! We must get him back to camp."

Jim and three men helped Tom back to camp. Jim dressed the wound as gently as he could. Tom made no outcry, but beads of sweat rolled down his face.

It was late in the evening when Jim joined the men at the campfires. "How is Tom?" they asked.

"He will be all right," answered Jim, "but his hand is crippled for life."

"How did it happen?"

"Tom isn't sure," replied Jim. "He knows he didn't use enough gunpowder to make the gun explode."

"Maybe the bullet in his gun rolled toward the muzzle just as he fired," spoke up a trapper.

"That could happen, and if it did Tom's lucky to be alive," said Provot. "An explosion like that could have killed him."

"That's what I tried to tell him," said Jim. "But now he's worrying about how long it will take him to get used to a new gun. You know how he was about that old rifle of his. But then we're all alike when it comes to our guns."

The men nodded. "That's right," they agreed.

Next to his horse the trapper loved his gun. Often he would travel hundreds of miles to have his gun repaired by an expert. He was so used to the weight, the length of the barrel, the feel of the wooden stock that the gun seemed a part of him. He spent hours cleaning and oiling it. He polished it to a dull finish so that in the sunlight no flashes of light would betray him to the Indians.

Tom's accident gained a new name for him among the Indians. They called him "Broken Hand," and as his fame spread throughout the West wherever the Indians, hostile or friendly, spoke of "Broken Hand," it was always with great respect.

The rendezvous was a success. General Ashley and Jed had sold or traded all their goods at high prices. They had almost two hundred packs of fine furs to take back to St. Louis.

"If we are as successful the next two years, Jed," said the general, "I plan to retire from the fur trade. I'm going back into politics. I may run for Congress. Why don't you retire, too?"

"And leave the West?" questioned Jed. "I

couldn't do it. Something holds me out here."

"It's a dangerous life, Jed. Three out of five trappers lose their lives here in the West." Ashley placed a hand on Jed's shoulder. "Don't wait too long, my friend. The odds are against you."

"I know it," answered Jed, "but I'll take my chances."

*   *   *

In 1826 General Ashley, having made his fortune, retired from the fur trade. He became one of the most important men in Missouri. He was elected to Congress. He served the people of his state with the same fine ability that had won for him the highest praise of the fur trappers of the Old West.

———

1. Name some of the beaver signs that were familiar to the trappers.
2. What does "rendezvous" mean?
3. Tell about the first rendezvous.
4. Tell why Jim's fur packs were the best.
5. How many beaver skins were in a fur pack?
6. How much did a pack weigh?
7. Why did the Indians call Tom Fitzpatrick, "Broken Hand"?

The Odds Are against You

JED SMITH'S new partners were Bill Sublette and Davy Jackson. The trappers were pleased. Although they respected General Ashley and Major Henry, the new owners were men from their own ranks.

"This is the chance we need to prove what we young men can do in the West," said Tom.

"We'll prove that we can get along by ourselves," spoke up Jim, "and we'll have the time of our lives doing it."

Only Provot and a few men did not remain with the old group of trappers. The rest of the men, however, formed their parties and set out to trap and explore.

During the next few years they trapped in almost every region of the West. They were proud of the many fine furs, the Ashley Beaver, they brought back with them.

Jed Smith, always eager to see new lands, spent most of his time exploring. He blazed two trails to the Pacific. His northwest route over the mountains was easier and more central than the route mapped out by earlier explorers.

Jed made two trips to California, the almost unknown land belonging to Mexico. He made both trips by traveling southwest in order to avoid the terrible strain of crossing the Sierra Nevada Mountains. But the southwestern trips were just as difficult for he had to cross the Mohave Desert.

Jed's explorations did not open new trapping territory and at first little value was placed upon them. His discoveries were not fully appreciated until the California gold rush in 1849. Then thousands of gold seekers swept into golden, sunny California. Jed Smith, the pathfinder, had blazed the trails for them.

Of more value to the trappers were their own explorations in search of beaver streams. Jim's discovery of Great Salt Lake had opened up the Great Salt Lake Valley. The valley to the west was a barren wasteland which was unimportant to the trappers. But in the eastern part of the valley they found many beaver streams.

Following the streams, the men pushed on searching—ever searching for richer fields. Far and wide they roamed, and soon the new lands held no secrets from them.

The years passed quickly and the men shared many exciting adventures. Early each summer they held a rendezvous. Several thousand Indians and trappers attended the annual meetings. Rival fur traders came, too. But when the trading was over most of the fur packs belonged to the Smith, Jackson, and Sublette Company.

The rendezvous in 1830 was held on the eastern side of the Rockies in a valley near South Pass. Although the trappers and Indians started coming to the valley early in July, the trading did not begin until the middle of the month. The men had to wait for Bill Sublette to arrive from St. Louis with the trading goods.

When he finally reached the rendezvous the white men were almost as surprised as the Indians. Bill had brought the goods in ten covered wagons, each drawn by ten mules. It was the first time wagons had crossed the plains over the familiar trail used by the trappers. This trail was to become the famous Oregon Trail.

Few Indians had seen wheels or anything on wheels before. They stared in wonder at the big wagons. And days later, the trading and feasting over, they left, still shaking their heads at the strange ways of the white men.

The 1830 rendezvous was important for another reason. Having made a fortune in the fur trade, Smith, Jackson, and Sublette sold their company to five of the best trappers in the outfit. The new owners were Jim, Tom, Milton, and two older men.

"You and your friends earned this break, Jim," said an old-timer, slapping Jim on the back. "We're all for you. Say, Tom," he called, "come here."

As Tom joined them, the old-timer asked, "Do you remember when Jim didn't even know what 'up to beaver' meant?"

Jim and Tom roared with laughter.

"Let's see. That was eight years ago, back in 1822. You boys have come a long way since then, and you have had a lot of hard times, too."

"Yes, we have," Tom agreed, "but it's been worth it, hasn't it, Jim?"

"Worth it!" Jim exclaimed. "I wouldn't trade places with anyone in the world."

Later that evening the men were seated around a campfire.

"Where are you planning to trap this fall?" asked Jed turning to Tom.

"We're going back to Three Forks."

"Stay away from the Blackfeet," warned Bill. "They will only make trouble for you."

"No, this time we're going back fully prepared," spoke up Jim. "I've never forgotten the fur packs those redskins took from us."

"Well, all right, boys," laughed Bill. "It's your company. By the way, what are you naming the company?"

"The Rocky Mountain Fur Company," answered Jim. "Remember that was the name Ashley and Henry used when we were all greenhorns."

"Well, fellows, what are your plans?" asked Tom. "Are you planning to retire?"

"Indeed not!" exclaimed Jed. "We're going to try our luck as traders in the Mexican territory of the Southwest. We're going to follow the Santa Fe Trail."

"We should make a lot of money," spoke up Bill. "The Mexicans are eager to buy all kinds of American goods and they will pay high prices to get them. This coming spring we're taking a wagon train of supplies to Santa Fe, New Mexico. We'll sell silks and velvets and—"

"Silks and velvets!" exclaimed Jim.

The men roared with laughter.

"We'll have other supplies, too," said Davy. "Traps, guns, and ammunition for the trappers who use Santa Fe and Taos as their headquarters."

"It's big business," said Jed, "but the best thing about it is that the Southwest is new country to me."

Jim laughed. "And that's what made you decide to go into the Santa Fe trade."

"I'll admit it helped," grinned Jed.

A few days later Jed, Bill, and Davy left for St. Louis with almost two hundred fur packs. As the wagons disappeared over the top of a hill Jim said, "They can have the Santa Fe Trail and their silks and velvets. This is where I belong—here in the Rocky Mountains."

With Tom as captain and Jim second-in-command, the trappers headed for Three Forks. Nearing the land of the bloody Blackfeet the scouts reported many hostile signs. Brave as the trappers were many of them wanted to turn back. Only when Jim took over the scouting duties were they willing to go on.

Jim, riding Wasaka, was happy to be scouting again. It was the job he loved best. Everywhere he found signs of the Blackfeet. He knew they were watching, waiting to hurl a surprise attack against his party.

But for once the Blackfeet were cautious. They did not attack. Two hundred well-armed trappers were not easy to surprise. In time the Indians gave up hope of catching the white men off guard.

Nevertheless, they followed every move of the party. They began to leave false signs along the trail to trick the white men's scout. Lying in wait, they watched to see if Jim would race back to his men.

At first the Indians were angry when Jim spotted the signs and, after examining them, rode on. Then, although they hated him, they could not help but admire him. In spite of themselves the cool courage of the lone scout won their respect.

The trapping around Three Forks was excellent. The men had many fur packs before they started southward again. Following a stream they came to South Pass, crossed it and traveled on to the Great Salt Lake Valley. After trapping here for several weeks they returned to the pass and headed for the Powder River Valley where they planned to spend the winter. During the fall season the men had ridden more than a thousand miles.

The winter months passed much too slowly to suit the men. But at last the first signs of spring came to the valley. The trappers with Jim again as their scout made for the mountains.

In April, Tom turned the command of the party over to Milton. Tom and another trapper left at once for St. Louis. Tom was to buy the trading goods needed for the summer rendezvous.

After days of steady travel Tom and his companion reached St. Louis. Almost the first men Tom saw were his three friends, Jed, Bill, and Davy. They urged him to go with them to Santa Fe.

"I can't," Tom said. "I'm here to buy supplies for our rendezvous in the Green River Valley."

"Come with us and we'll sell you all the supplies you need," said Bill.

"It's out of my way. I'd be almost as far from the Green in Santa Fe as I am now in St. Louis."

Jed laughed. "What difference does it make? Come on, Tom. We'll get you to your rendezvous on time and we'll haul the supplies for nothing."

"Well, I could stop at Taos and sign up some good men to trap for the company," said Tom. "All right, boys, I'll go. By the way, what do you know about the Santa Fe Trail?"

Jed shook his head. "We don't know very much about it. The traders tell me that the trip across the Cimarron Desert is the hardest part of the trail. But I've crossed the Mohave Desert and so I'm not worried about the Cimarron."

"What about the Indians?" asked Tom.

"Well, the Pawnees and the Comanches are not friendly."

Tom laughed. "We're used to that, aren't we?"

"Now that you have decided to go with us, I advise you to buy a brace of revolvers like mine," Jed said. He touched the pair of silver-mounted revolvers he wore in a belt buckled around his slim waist. "You'll need them on the Santa Fe."

"All right. I'll buy a pair," said Tom. "How soon are we getting started?"

"We're leaving for Independence, Missouri, to-morrow. That's where the Santa Fe Trail begins now. We're buying all our supplies there instead of in St. Louis as it will save us hauling the goods about three hundred miles."

It was early in May when the caravan of twenty wagons and eighty men left the trading-post town of Independence. The wagon train set out across the prairie. The trail was easy to follow. Hundreds of wagon trains had made the trip before and the wagon wheels had cut deep ruts in the ground.

The trail, some eight hundred miles long, was almost a direct route to Santa Fe. The directness of the route showed how well the explorers of the Old West had blazed their trails.

The trail was in American territory until it reached the fork of the Arkansas River. The remaining half was through land belonging to Mexico.

The caravan traveled from eighteen to twenty miles a day. Slowly the well-watered grassy prairie gave way to a dry, barren region. The trail was harder to follow and the landmarks were fewer. But the men rode on. They were confident, as all mountain men were, of their ability to cross any kind of country.

When they reached the fork of the Arkansas River the Cimarron Desert lay ahead of them—sixty miles of wasteland!

The caravan halted to rest the horses and mules. The men filled many casks with water for the trip across the desert. Then, they pushed on. They had gone only a few miles when they knew that the trip would be very difficult.

There were no landmarks and it was impossible to follow the trail. The soil was so dry and hard that only a few tracks of other wagon wheels were left to guide them.

The heat was intense. The men traveled slowly to spare their animals. The water supply was used in a few days and small parties of men went out to search for water holes. They found none. The suffering of the thirsty men and animals became almost unbearable.

The men at last broke down. "We can't go on," they said. "We must have water."

"Tom, let's try to find a water hole," said Jed. "Maybe by some miracle we'll find one."

The two men, weak and parched with thirst, mounted their horses and rode away. They followed one of the countless buffalo paths which crossed and recrossed the desert. They knew that buffalo paths at certain times of the year often led to water holes. Mile after mile they rode, urging their stumbling horses along. At last hoping that one of them would find water they decided to separate.

"I'll meet you here in an hour," said Jed. He leaned from his saddle and placed a hand on Tom's shoulder.

Without another word Jed rode southward. He came to the top of a low hill and turned in his saddle. He waved his broad-brimmed hat. Tom returned the old familiar salute of the trail. Then, with his hat still held high, Jed and his horse disappeared from view.

Tom rested his weary horse for a little while and then slowly headed westward. An hour later he returned, even more slowly, to the spot where he was to meet Jed.

"I hope he had better luck than I," Tom thought.

At first he waited quietly. When Jed did not return, however, Tom became alarmed. He rode south to meet him. There was no trace of Jed or his horse.

"Maybe he found a water hole and has ridden back to the caravan," Tom said to himself as he turned his horse around. When he reached the caravan he learned that Jed had not returned.

"He's lost!" exclaimed Bill.

"Not Jed," said Tom. "Something has happened to him. Come, men, we must find him."

Forgetting their thirst and thinking now only of Jed, the men spread out to search for him. Hours later they met again. None had found any trace of Jed nor of his horse.

"I found a water hole," one man reported. "It's almost dry but by digging into the earth we can get enough water to survive while we search for Jed."

For three days the men searched, but they found no trace of Jed. Finally they gave up hope. Slowly, sadly the caravan traveled on to Santa Fe.

The day after their arrival Tom went with Bill and Davy to a trading post. While Bill and Davy were talking to the merchant, Tom looked over the goods on display. He stopped beside a case filled with revolvers.

His eyes widened and he felt the blood drain from his face. With trembling hands he reached for a pair of silver-mounted revolvers.

"They're Jed's!" he cried. "Where did you get them?" he demanded of the merchant.

Before the man could answer Bill and Davy saw

the revolvers. "Jed's!" they exclaimed in one voice.

"Where did you get them?" Tom asked again.

"A trader sold them to me," answered the merchant. "He got them from a band of Comanche Indians. They killed a white man on the Cimarron Desert. Why?" he asked as the three men turned quickly away.

"The white man was our friend," said Tom.

"What was his name?" asked the merchant.

"Jed Smith."

"Jed Smith, the mountain man?"

Tom nodded.

"I have already promised to sell them to someone, but as you were a friend of Jed Smith's," said the merchant, "I'm glad to give them to you."

"Thanks, thanks a lot," replied Tom. He turned to Bill and Davy. "We'll give them to Jim. Jed would like that, wouldn't he?"

"Yes," they answered, "Jed would like that."

———

1. Why did the trappers spend so much time exploring?
2. How did the discoveries help the settlers?
3. Tell about the Santa Fe Trail.

Trouble in the Mountains

SEVERAL MONTHS later Tom rejoined his fellow trappers in the West. Davy and Bill did not come with him. They had, however, sold him all the trading goods he needed. They had also promised to bring the supplies to next year's rendezvous. On the way Tom had stopped at the little Mexican town of Taos. He had hired fifty men to trap for the company and had brought them with him.

As soon as he arrived Tom told the trappers that Jed had been killed on the Cimarron Desert. At first they did not believe it.

Jim, holding the silver-mounted revolvers, kept saying, "It can't be true. It just couldn't happen to Jed."

The trappers were used to the dangers which, in a split second, could snuff out a man's life. But the news of Jed's death stunned them. He had been a mountain man—a friend to all.

Friendship was more than a word to the mountain men. It was a real living part of their daily lives. They had no courts of law and order. But few men lived by sterner, more exacting rules of conduct. Their laws, the code of the West, soon weeded out all cheats and cowards. Here, a man's word, courage, and honor were all that counted. Few men gave more proof of their friendship to one another than the mountain men of the Old West.

And Jed had been one of the best of them. Now, remembering him, the strong men wept and were not ashamed of their tears.

"That new trapper over there reminds me of Jed," said Tom pointing to a slender, buckskin-clad young man. "His name is Kit Carson."

For a while Jim and the rest of the trappers resented Kit for he was very much like Jed. His blue eyes had Jed's keen, steady gaze. He spoke quietly, softly, and he was modest, almost shy, like Jed. But Kit soon won the friendship of the trappers. He, too, lived by the code of the West.

During the fall trapping season Jim scouted for the party. One morning when he mounted

Wasaka he noticed Tom and Kit watching him.
"What's the matter?" he called to them.

"Nothing," Tom replied. "Kit was just telling
me that he intends to be a scout."

"Have you done any scouting?" asked Jim.

"A little," Kit answered.

"Get your horse and come with me," said Jim.

Jim and Kit were soon on their way. They kept
their horses at a steady, even gallop. Once Kit
was about to speak, but a glance at Jim stopped
him. In camp Jim was always laughing and talking. But on the trail he was silent. He rode leaning forward in his saddle, one hand holding Wasaka's reins lightly and the other on his rifle. He
appeared to look neither to the right nor left. But
his eyes were everywhere, searching for signs
along the trail.

After they had ridden several miles they halted
to rest their horses. Jim questioned Kit about the
trail. Kit had missed some signs. He admitted it
quickly and did not try to excuse himself.

"I certainly missed the chance I've been waiting
for and I have only myself to blame," said Kit. He

shook his head and added, "I signed up to trap for your company because I thought I would get a chance to learn how to scout from you."

"Anyone could have missed those signs."

"You didn't."

"That's different," Jim laughed. "I know the country. It's new to you."

"But the signs are the same anywhere."

"Maybe I was riding too fast."

"You don't waste any time," Kit replied. "How can you follow a trail so quickly, or is that a secret like your castor bait?"

"No, my scouting is not a secret," answered Jim. "I'll be glad to teach you everything I know. We need good scouts. I want to help you, Kit, because I think you can be one of the best."

All during the fall Jim and Kit rode together. Kit was determined to become a good scout. He listened intently to Jim's advice and willingly carried out his orders. Seldom did Jim have to explain more than once any sign they found along the trail.

Jim was generous in his praise of Kit's ability. And Kit, like the greenhorns whom Jim had brought "up to beaver," was devoted to him.

When winter set in the men hurried to the nearest mountain valley, "Jackson Hole," named for Davy Jackson. A hole, as the trappers called a mountain valley, was a good place to camp for the winter months.

Beautiful Jackson Hole in the Teton Mountains was one of their favorite spots. Here they found everything they needed, water from the mountain streams, wood for their campfires, grass for their horses, and a plentiful supply of game.

On the western side of the Tetons was another mountain valley called "Pierre's Hole." The trappers decided to hold the annual rendezvous there when the spring trapping season was ended.

As usual, life in the winter camp made the men restless. Surrounded by the snowcapped peaks of the mighty Tetons they longed to be on the move again. And this year they were even more anxious to get an early start.

Other fur companies were sending out more men each year. At first the Rocky Mountain Fur Company trappers were not worried for they, ever exploring, pushed on to richer beaver territory. And for a while the rivals were left behind.

Then the American Fur Company began to cause trouble. The leaders of their trapping parties did not bother to explore the land. They simply followed the trails of the men who already knew the West, the Rocky Mountain Fur Company trappers. The newcomers were shrewd business men. In a few years the wealthy American Fur Company was the most powerful company in the West.

"They want to control the fur trade," said Tom. "They may do it, too. They are able business men."

"I know it and I'm worried," spoke up Milton. "As they become stronger we and other small companies will have a harder time."

"Well, I'm worried, too," said Jim, "but we won't get anywhere by talking about it. Let's get out and do some trapping. They may break us, but let's give them a race they won't forget."

Once on the trail the men forgot their worries. This was the life they understood. All spring they kept on the move. Then as the season ended they headed for Pierre's Hole for their rendezvous.

When they reached the Hole they were met by the men of the American Fur Company. The rivals had already begun trading with the Indians.

"They act as if this were their rendezvous," said Milton angrily.

"We still have a chance," Tom said. "Most of the Indians and free trappers won't get here for several weeks. By that time Bill should be here with our trading goods."

"If Bill doesn't make it, we're finished," spoke up Jim. "But if we could get word to him that we are in trouble, he'd be here on time."

"He ought to be almost across the plains by now," said Tom. "I'll ride east and find him somewhere along the trail. It will be a long hard trip, but it's our only chance."

An hour later Tom, Kit Carson and four other men were on their way. Each man had two horses so that when riding one horse the other would be fresh for the next stretch. Each man carried plenty of ammunition and a week's food supply.

Following a short cut about which Jim had told him, Tom headed his party toward South Pass. The men rode swiftly, sparing neither their horses nor themselves. They rode until they ached with weariness and almost fell from their saddles. They stopped only long enough to catch a few hours' sleep and then rode on. Day after day they kept up the steady pace. Most of the time they were too tired to eat, too tired to sleep. But none complained, for they were mountain men.

After a four-hundred-mile ride they met Bill and his sixty men, and one hundred and eighty pack animals loaded with trading goods. Bill needed no urging to hurry on to the rendezvous.

"We knew you would help us," said Tom. "Now I must get back to the rendezvous as quickly as I can. I'll ride with your train to the Sweetwater. Then I'll go on alone."

A few days later the men came into the valley of the Sweetwater. Tom said good-by to his friends and rode on. He had two horses, but this time instead of riding first one horse and then the other, he did not change. The extra horse, saddled and bridled, must be kept fresh to be used if he were chased by Indians.

The familiar trail up the Sweetwater was easy to follow.

Tom had no trouble until he crossed South Pass and was riding along a stream in the Green River Valley. Late one afternoon he sighted a band of Blackfeet Indians. At the same moment the Indians saw him. They raced toward him yelling and waving their tomahawks.

In a flash Tom mounted his fresh horse. Leaning low over his saddle he whirled the horse about and galloped back to a mountain path.

For a time Tom kept his lead over the Indians. But the path was rough and steep, and slowly the horse weakened under the strain. The yelling Indians began to gain on him.

The horse stumbled and fell. As the horse struggled to rise Tom searched for a hiding place. Some distance up the mountain slope he saw a hole in a rock. Tucking his rifle under his arm he scrambled up the slope.

As he ran he gathered up an armful of leaves and sticks. Quickly he crawled into the hole and covered the opening with the leaves and sticks.

From the shouts of the Indians he could tell they had found his horse. "And now they will spread out and look for me," he said to himself.

All afternoon the Indians searched but they did not find Tom. Twice the braves were so near his hiding place Tom could have touched them. Once in spite of himself he grinned as a brave said, "Must be Indian we hunt. White man not hide so good."

When it was almost dark the Indians gave up the search. Tom did not leave the hole. Patiently he waited to be certain that no Indian guards were near by. The hours dragged on and on.

"Now I'll try to escape," he said crawling out of the hole. He stretched to ease his stiff muscles. Then slowly he made his way down the mountain.

He looked up at the stars and set his course by the North Star. Shouldering his rifle Tom headed for the rendezvous.

Suddenly the barking of dogs broke the stillness of the night. For a minute Tom stood motionless. "Dogs! I'm in the Indians' camp," he thought. "Now I'm in for it."

Running as fast as he could Tom returned to his hiding place. His buckskin clothes were torn and he had cut his hands on the rocks. But he was safe.

In the morning the Indians were out searching for him again. All day the braves shouted to one another as they scrambled up and down the steep slopes. Late in the afternoon the chief, riding Tom's horse, led his braves back to their camp.

Once again in the darkness Tom tried to escape. He circled wide and slipped by the Indians' camp. With the North Star as his guide he walked all night. As morning dawned he found another hiding place and hid during the day. That night he was on his way again.

In the morning he was very hungry. He wanted to shoot a buffalo, but he dared not fire his rifle. He was still too near the Indians. Instead he hunted for berries and roots and ate them.

He came to a mountain stream. It was too wide for him to swim so he made a crude raft. Halfway across the stream the raft broke in two. His rifle was carried away by the rushing waters.

Somehow, more dead than alive, he reached the opposite bank.

Day after day Tom struggled on toward the rendezvous. The trip was becoming more and more difficult. His mocassins wore out and he cut up his big hat to make another pair. He was starving and although he searched for berries and roots he found only a few. He became so weak he could barely walk. He had to rest more often, but somehow he stumbled on.

Then one morning he was so weak he could no longer get to his feet. He crawled along the trail on his hands and knees. His hair dropped down over his shoulders and with unbelieving eyes he stared at his long hair. It had turned white—snow white.

Tom gritted his teeth and crawled on. At last, unable to go any farther, he fell forward. He lay still, his face in the dust of the trail.

Hours later, he never knew how long, he felt the touch of a hand on his shoulder. And as from a dream world he heard the voices of two Indians.

"Old man dead," the braves were saying. "We no help him. We go."

Tom forced himself to move his head. "No! No!" he thought he shouted, but he had barely whispered the words.

"He move!" the braves exclaimed as they knelt beside him. "He talk."

The Indians lifted Tom to a sitting position and for awhile talked in excited whispers.

"We feed old man," one brave said. "We camp here tonight."

"We go in morning," the other Indian replied. "We have no time. White men at rendezvous send us hunt for Broken Hand."

"I'm Broken Hand," Tom whispered.

"No! No!" the Indians protested. "Broken Hand big fine man. We know. He our friend."

Slowly Tom raised his crippled hand.

The Indians looked at each other and then at Tom. They touched his hand.

"Broken Hand!" they shouted. "We find you!"

The Indians made camp. Gently they cared for Tom. They fed him and gave him new buckskin clothes and moccasins. Tom tried to thank them for saving his life, but the braves told him to rest. All night they took turns sitting beside him as he slept.

In the morning after feeding Tom, the Indians lifted him onto a horse. With a brave holding him in the saddle they started back to the rendezvous. They traveled slowly for Tom was still very weak.

At last they reached Pierre's Hole. The rendezvous was over, but the trappers and many Indians were still there. They were shocked to see

Tom. But they were happy and thankful that he was still alive.

Shouts of "Tom" and "Broken Hand" rang out as mountain men and Indians crowded around him.

"Tom, you are all right, aren't you?" Jim and Milton asked as they half-carried, half-walked Tom to a campfire.

"Sure, I'm all right," Tom answered. "What about Bill?" he asked. "Did he get here on time?"

"I certainly did," said Bill as he sat down beside Tom. "I wish you could have seen those traders of the American Fur Company when I arrived."

"We had a fine season," said Milton.

"Good!" Tom smiled weakly. He turned to Jim. "What's the matter, Jim?" he asked. "You're so quiet."

"There's nothing the matter now, Tom," replied Jim. "You're here and that's all that counts. We're together again."

---

1. What was the code of the mountain men?
2. Discuss with the class why rules of conduct as well as laws are necessary.
3. Name three rules of conduct which you think would make a good code.

The Trails Have Been Blazed

THE YEARS rolled over the plains and the mountains. The men of the Rocky Mountain Fur Company continued to trap, fight Indians, and hold their annual rendezvous.

A change, however, was coming into their lives. After years of constant trapping, the beaver supply was becoming exhausted. And there were now many other fur companies in the West.

Each year the men marked fewer fur packs with their old familiar brand, "R. M. F. Co." At first they were not greatly concerned. There was no real cause for worry as long as the price of beaver pelts remained high.

But as the years passed the number of fur packs steadily decreased. And then—the prices began to fall.

The small companies were unable to pay their men and buy the supplies needed for trading with the Indians and free trappers. One by one they sold out to the rival they all hated and feared, the American Fur Company.

But with all its power and great wealth its traders could not buy the Rocky Mountain Fur Company. That was the one company its traders tried to ruin because they wanted the Rocky Mountain men to trap for their company.

In 1834, the two older trappers who owned the Rocky Mountain Fur Company with Jim, Tom, and Milton became discouraged and quit. The rest of the men were stubbornly loyal. They refused to quit. They signed up to trap for the new firm of "Fitzpatrick, Sublette, and Bridger."

From the start the odds were against the little company. Two years later the men held their last rendezvous in the mountains.

It was not the great wealth and power of their rival that finally crushed the men of the Rocky Mountain Fur Company. Nor was it the Indians who defeated them. It was a hat—a silk hat!

For years the men in the United States and in Europe had worn the tall hats made of beaver fur.

In some years, as many as two hundred thousand beaver skins were shipped to Europe. The fur trade had depended almost entirely upon the sale of beaver pelts.

Then in Paris, France, a man began making hats of silk. In a few years the silk hats were the accepted style.

The great days of the fur trade were ended. There was still a demand for some beaver pelts and the skins of other fur-bearing animals. But it was no longer big business. Only a wealthy company could afford to send its trappers into the wilderness.

Backed by millions of dollars the American Fur Company took over the fur trade. Its traders selected the best trappers, but hired them at lower wages. The men accepted the lower wages for they needed work and trapping was the job they understood and loved.

The traders were anxious to hire the men of the famous old Rocky Mountain Fur Company. But Jim, Tom, Milton, and their trappers had left the mountains. They had returned to their little fort on the Laramie River. They had recently purchased the fort from Bill Sublette.

The men were a discouraged lot. Their business was ruined. They had only a few supplies left. Milton was seriously ill. Tom had gone to St. Louis with Bill to sell their last fur packs. As always the men turned to Jim.

"We'll get by somehow," he said to them. "As long as there is any trapping to be done here in the West we will trap. Maybe not for ourselves," he added, "but for the American Fur Company."

"Their traders hired many men at the rendezvous," reminded a trapper. "They didn't hire us."

"They wanted to hire us," replied Jim. "I refused to accept the lower wages they offered us."

He looked at his discouraged, loyal men. Their buckskin clothes were black from the smoke of many campfires. Their faces were tanned by the wind and sun. Danger had made their eyes keen and searching. They were men—real men.

"You will all be trapping again," he said at last. "An American trader will hire you because you're the best of the mountain men."

The men crowded around him. "Thanks, Jim," they said over and over. Hard, rough hands slapped him on the shoulder. "Thanks, Jim."

A few days later an American Fur Company trader arrived at the fort. Jim greeted him in his usual friendly manner.

"I've been expecting you," he said. "You still want to hire us to trap for your company."

"You're right," the trader laughed.

"Have you changed your mind about the wages for our men?" asked Jim.

"We are hiring good trappers for less money this year. We will pay your men the same as we pay the others. But we'll pay you and Tom more—"

"Tom and I are not interested in what you will pay us," broke in Jim. "But we are both interested in what will happen to our men."

"Well, now, Bridger," protested the trader, "your men can't expect good wages in times like these. We will pay you and Tom whatever you ask. We want you, Bridger, in command of all our trapping parties. We have over six hundred men ready and waiting to follow your orders."

"What about Tom?"

"We want to buy this fort from you. We have other trading posts but this fort will be our main trading post in the West. We want Tom to be in charge of it. And when Milton is well again he can work here with Tom."

"But what about our men?" Jim asked again.

"We'll pay them the same wages as our other trappers."

"Then count us out of this deal," said Jim. "Tom and I won't work for your company unless our men are treated fairly. That's final."

The trader drew a deep breath. "All right, Bridger, you win. I was told to hire you no matter what I had to pay. It's taken us a long time to get the Rocky Mountain men."

"And all because of a silk hat," Jim sighed a little. "A silk hat!"

When Tom returned from St. Louis he took over command of the fort. Jim and the trappers were busy getting ready to leave for the mountains. But for Milton there was nothing to do.

"I'm not much help any more," he said to Jim and Tom one day. "I'm sorry, boys."

"Sorry!" exclaimed Jim trying to hide his true feelings. He knew that Milton would not get well. "Why, in no time you'll be telling Tom how to run the fort."

"Sure you will," agreed Tom quickly.

"No," Milton shook his head. "You both know better and so do I. I've used up all my luck. I didn't go back to St. Louis with Bill because this is where I want to die—here in the West I love."

The three good friends were silent. At last Milton asked, "When do you leave, Jim?"

"In the morning."

"I'll miss you, but I'm glad that Tom will be here with me."

"I'll be back," Jim promised. "As soon as I can, I'll be back."

Jim and his men met the other trappers in the mountains. Jim gave his orders to the captains and scouts. The parties spread out and the fall trapping season was on.

It was a good season even though none of the

parties brought in as many fur packs as in the old days. The men cached their packs and headed for the Powder River Valley to spend the winter.

Jim hurried back to the little fort on the Laramie. There one December day, Milton died. Jim and Tom were with him.

Jim spent the rest of the winter at the fort. In the spring he rejoined his trappers. For the next few years he remained in command of the fur trapping parties of the American Fur Company.

But each summer he was free to do as he wished. Then, with Tom or an Indian friend, but more often alone, he roamed the West. He remembered everything he saw. He knew the Indians living on both sides of the Rockies.

Tom was in charge of a new and much larger trading post on the Laramie. It was known as "Fort Laramie" and it was to become one of the most famous forts in all the West. The Indians for miles around came to trade at the fort. When Tom resigned from the company and left for St. Louis, the Indians were sad. They thought he was going back there to live.

But Tom was not leaving the West. In the summer of 1841 he returned with a party of missionaries and the first settlers headed for California.

Jim was at the fort. He was glad to see Tom and to meet John Bidwell who had planned the first overland trip to California.

Later Jim said to Tom, "I wish Jed had lived to meet that fine young man." He touched the silver-mounted revolvers he always wore around his waist. "Jed said that some day the settlers would come. And here they are. Here they are."

Tom nodded. "Yes, this is the first of the thousands of settlers who will come to build the West."

"We are ready for them," smiled Jim. "The trails have been blazed."

Jim watched as the covered wagons rolled on in a cloud of dust. The march to the West had begun. And Tom Fitzpatrick, the fur trapper, was leading the way.

Jim was determined to do his share. He decided to build a fort, a trading post. It would be like the other forts in the West, a group of buildings surrounded by a high stockade. But there would be one difference. The other forts had been built as trading centers for the Indians and trappers. Jim planned to build a fort to help the settlers.

Where should he build the fort? It must be on the trail the settlers would use. Knowing the West better than any other man he decided to build his fort in the Green River Valley.

It was the valley he loved best. But more important it was where the settlers would need help. When they reached the Green they would have traveled more than a thousand miles from St. Louis. After the difficult trip across the plains and over South Pass they would need supplies and a chance to rest. Then they would push on to California or on to the Oregon country.

In the Green River Valley, Jim built his fort and welcomed the oncoming settlers. At the fort they found all the supplies they needed. But best of all there was Jim with his ready smile and friendly advice.

Year after year more settlers came to the West. They all stopped at famous "Fort Bridger." Many times they did not have enough money to pay for their supplies. It did not matter to Jim. He let them have everything they needed. He never failed them. He was their friend.

One day Tom and a party of settlers arrived at the fort. The two friends talked for hours.

"Do you still have Wasaka?" Tom asked.

"Oh, yes," Jim laughed, "and he acts as if he owned the valley. He's too old to ride any more," he added, "so I just let him graze. But Wasaka is still the best horse in the West. The settlers' children think so, too. I tell them a lot of stories about the old days when Wasaka and I followed the beaver streams."

"Have you had many settlers here this summer?"

"Well, one of my clerks is keeping a record. He has already listed the names of more than fifteen thousand men, women, and children."

"You're doing all right, aren't you, Jim?"

"Yes, but I want to get back on the trail."

"What will become of the fort, Jim? The settlers depend upon getting supplies here."

"My clerks can run the fort without me. I can

do more good now by being a scout or a guide for a wagon train."

"The settlers need experienced leaders on the trip across the plains and mountains," replied Tom. "Most of them are as green as grass. They haven't the faintest idea of the dangers and hardships of the trail. At first they think they can get along by themselves. But after an Indian attack or buffalo stampede, they're very glad to carry out the orders of an old-timer."

"You know, Tom, when a wagon train nears the fort I watch it closely. If it's in good condition I know one of our men of the old Rocky Mountain Fur Company is in command."

"Our trappers were the best of the mountain men," said Tom. "They should be the best of the scouts and guides. And with you in the saddle again, Jim, it will be like the good old days." He paused. "No, those days are gone forever. But the years ahead will be even better."

Jim looked across the valley. Far away a covered wagon train rolled toward the fort. "You're right, Tom. The years ahead will be even better. The wilderness no longer belongs to us. It now belongs to the settlers—the builders of our nation."

*   *   *   *

The story of the fur trade in the Old West is a record of the brave deeds and stout courage of its men, the mountain men. There were less than a thousand men engaged in the western fur trade. But they blazed the trails for the tens of thousands of settlers who built the West.

And of all the men, the Rocky Mountain Fur Company trappers were the best. They opened up the richest trapping lands. Their discoveries and exploring trips were the most important. They were the best of the scouts and guides during the covered-wagon days. Many were killed in pitched battles with the Indians. Others sleep in lonely, unmarked graves.

High in the list of the famous old company trappers stand the names of Jim Bridger, Tom Fitzpatrick, Jed Smith, Bill and Milton Sublette. They are remembered, for they blazed their trails when the odds were against them.

Word List